To Andrew Taylor,
who introduced me to muesli in Harlesden

Nothing that you will learn in the course of your studies will be of the slightest possible use to you in after life—save only this—that if you work hard and diligently you should be able to detect when a man is talking rot, and that, in my view, is the main, if not the sole, purpose of education.

—J. A. Smith

Jeremiad Interviews

Blaise Cronin

The Scarecrow Press, Inc.
Lanham, Maryland, and Oxford
2004

SCARECROW PRESS, INC.

Published in the United States of America
by Scarecrow Press, Inc.
A wholly owned subsidiary of
The Rowman & Littlefield Publishing Group, Inc.
4501 Forbes Boulevard, Suite 200, Lanham, Maryland 20706
www.scarecrowpress.com

PO Box 317
Oxford
OX2 9RU, UK

British Library Cataloguing in Publication Information Available

Library of Congress Cataloging-in-Publication Data

Cronin, Blaise.
  Jeremiad Jottings / Blaise Cronin.
    p.   cm.
  Includes bibliographical references.
  ISBN 0-8108-4951-8 (alk. paper)
  1. Library science.   2. Information science.   3. Political
correctness–United States.   4. Education, Higher–Political
aspects–United States.   5. United States–Intellectual life–20th
century.   6. United States–Intellectual life–21st century.   I. Title.
Z665 .C779   2004
020—dc22   2003015310

♾ ™The paper used in this publication meets the minimum
requirements of American National Standard for Information
Sciences—Permanence of Paper for Printed Library Materials,
ANSI/NISO Z39.48-1992. Manufactured in the United States
of America.

CONTENTS

CREDITS

The works listed immediately hereafter appeared originally in *Library Journal* (in some cases with very minor changes as a result of copyediting decisions). They are reprinted here with permission and are copyright 2002 and 2003 Cahners Business Information, a division of Reed Elsevier Inc.: "What a Library Is Not," "Burned Any Good Books Lately?," "Follow the Money," "Coach Class in Academia," "*Can* You 'Celebrate' Diversity?," and "The Trouble with Trophy Speakers."

A version of "*Honoris Causa*" was published originally in *Academic Questions* (16, no. 1 [Winter 2002–03]: 60–68) and is reprinted here with permission of Transaction Publishers.

"Card Games" is a trivially edited version of "From Victorian Visiting Card to vCard: The Evolution of a Communicative Genre," authored by Blaise Cronin and Yvonne Rogers and published in the *Journal of Information Science* (29, no. 1 [2003]: 65–68). It is reprinted here with the permission of Cambridge Scientific Abstracts (CSA) and the Chartered Institute of Library and Information Professionals.

"Holding the Center" is an edited version of "Holding the Center While Prospecting at the Periphery: Domain Identity and Coherence in North American Information Studies Education," which was published in *Education for Information* (20, no. 1 [2002]: 3–10) and is reproduced here with permission of IOS Press.

"The Public Intellectual" is a slightly expanded version of a book review published in *Library Quarterly* (73, no. 1 [2003]: 78–

79) and is reproduced here with permission of the University of Chicago.

I am most grateful to Yvonne Rogers and Debora Shaw for taking the time to read drafts of the manuscript and also to Tiana Tew for her painstaking copyediting. Tone and content, along with any remaining errors and stylistic infelicities, are, of course, my responsibility alone.

PREFACE

I was going to call this collation *Son of Pulp Friction*, but I quickly thought better of the idea given the likely response from Libraryland's laptop-brandishing Amazons. The format of *Jeremiad Jottings* is, however, very similar to that of *Pulp Friction* (Cronin 2003), also published by Scarecrow Press; a batch of op-eds reprinted from my "Dean's List" column in *Library Journal*, combined with a miscellany of other essays, new and old. *Jeremiad Jottings* is an unrepentantly self-indulgent look at life in Libraryland and beyond, with the institutionally damaging effects of political correctness as the dominant leitmotif. "Beyond" includes the precious (in every sense of the word) world of the ivory tower (my natural habitat) where, as you will see, contortionist thinking and linguistic legerdemain have become distressingly à la mode. Although *Jeremiad Jottings* does not pretend to be a scholarly monograph, I have sprinkled it liberally with references, so the interested reader can pursue particular topics and perspectives. At the risk of stating the obvious, the book's somewhat dyspeptic tone should not mask the underlying seriousness of the issues I touch upon: the Barbarians are now well and truly inside the gates. And that is no laughing matter.

Truth be told, there was no formal plan or blueprint for the collection; I began by grabbing choice items from the flotsam of scholarly and professional life that washes daily across my desktop—things that raise one's eyebrows, strike a chord, offend one's sensibilities, insult logic, or invite parody. Of course, it is not entirely random; I do have a few familiar axes to grind, several shibboleths to slay. I'll gripe and I'll grouse (the title of the book demands no less), and I'll lampoon beloved institutions and individuals, but only because their actions and utterances sometimes merit such treatment. As Oscar Wilde once said, "There is no sin except stupidity." And sinning, as will soon become clear, is commonplace these days, especially at the highest tables of academia where "the ideologues of the multicultural and postmodern Left" are all too frequently seated (Hanson, Heath, and Thornton 2001, ix). Sadly, I am reminded daily of Peter Whittle's observation that "[p]olitical correctness has America by the throat, and nowhere is its grip tighter than in the entertainment industry here" (2003, 10). However, I would be inclined to substitute higher education for entertainment industry in this sentence.

And Libraryland is not far behind in the sinning stakes. The political antics of the American Library Association's (ALA) Social Responsibilities Round Table (SSRT) and its raft of task forces have been a source of bewilderment for many of us over the years, as, indeed, have the posturings of the parent itself (Cronin 1995). Most recently, we have had the unsightly spectacle of morally indignant librarians attempting to find a way around the (admittedly imperfect) USA PATRIOT Act by, for instance, destroying patron borrowing records on a daily basis to prevent them from falling into the hands of counterterrorism or law enforcement agents (Walfield 2003). It frequently seems as if developments and issues relevant to professional librarianship take a back seat to political activism and advocacy within the ranks of the ALA and its SSRT.

A colleague cheekily remarked that *Pulp Friction* was ideal reading material for the smallest room in the house. Not the most flattering of comments, perhaps, but I would rather have *Jeremiad Jottings* read there than wind up in a discount warehouse en route to the knacker's yard or gathering dust on the shelves of the Chattanooga Public Library. More boldly, my colleague Debora Shaw commented after reading a draft of the latest miscellany that she was "overwhelmed by its unremitting negativity," a reaction I didn't find wholly surprising. Nonetheless, it caused me to reflect. I duly considered retrofitting some niceties to offset the drumbeat of negatives, but, in the end, I thought the better of it. We all know that American libraries are wonderfully innovative in terms of their services, collection management policies, and use of information technologies. And who among us is not aware of the unmatched brilliance of this nation's university system?

However, what is less well understood is just how seriously these splendid institutions are threatened by the insidious presence of careerist ideologues and their fashionable cant. The Barbarians are, as I have said, inside the gates, and their weapon of choice is political correctness laced with doublespeak. In any event, I would rather have *Jeremiad Jottings* panned in print by conservatives and liberals alike than consigned to silence, which, since we are on the subject of the smallest room, reminds me of a remark made by the German composer, Max Reger, to a critic: "I am sitting in the smallest room of my house. I have your review before me. In a moment it will be behind me."

REFERENCES

Cronin, B. 1995. "Shibboleth and Substance in North American Library and Information Science Education." *Libri* 45, no. 1:45–63.

———. 2003. *Pulp Friction*. Lanham, Md.: Scarecrow Press.

Hanson, V. D., J. Heath, and B. S. Thornton. 2001. *Bonfire of the Humanities: Rescuing the Classics in an Impoverished Age*. Wilmington, Del.: ISI Books.

Walfield, P. 2003. "The ALA Library: Terrorist Sanctuary." *FrontPage-Magazine*. www.frontpagemag.com/Articles/Printable.asp?ID = 7704 [accessed 22 May 2003].

Whittle, P. 2003. "Censor Humour." *Sunday Times* (April 20): 1 (*Culture* section).

AFFIRMATIVE REACTION

How will the Supreme Court rule on the University of Michigan's use of racial preferences in admissions? As I write, it is one of the major talking points of the day, inside and well beyond academia. The issue is politically supercharged, the arguments complex, and the related emotions sometimes bellicose. In 1978 a divided Supreme Court ruled (Regents of the University of California vs. Bakke) that universities could treat race as a "plus factor" but could not use numerical quotas—a semantic sleight of hand worthy of medieval schoolmen. That, however, hasn't stopped some forty or so universities and many other organizations and institutions from filing *amici curiae* (friends of the court) briefs in support of Michigan's position. Indiana University (IU) is among the signatories, which is not altogether surprising given the IU Law School's vigorous and contentious commitment to affirmative action. By way of illustration, in 1999, the average LSAT score for black students at IU was 146, while the average for nonminority students was 159 (Mangan 2003).

The arguments driving the current debate are inextricably tied up with the history of segregation and institutional racism in the United States and the need for something nebulous called "diversity" on the nation's campuses (see the subsequent essay, *"Can You 'Celebrate' Diversity?"*). Both sides make compelling and sometimes moving arguments to support their respective positions, but all too often guilt and emotions cloud clear thinking. As an aside, Stanley Rothman (2003) found in his controversial survey of campus attitudes toward diversity that many faculty and administrators reject the use of racial or ethnic preferences. His investigation uncovered "silent opposition" among administrative ranks; almost half the administrators surveyed did not support admissions preferences. That, of course, does not mean that diversity may not be a good thing in educational contexts, though the National Association of Scholars, of which I am a member, would challenge such a view (see www.nas.org, "Race and Higher Education"), but it does, regrettably, show how political correctness can have a chilling effect on campus life and stifle discussion of sensitive issues.

The Michigan admission process awards a possible maximum of 150 points to would-be freshmen (Kantrowitz and Wingert 2003). Up to 110 points can be earned for academics, including 12 for standardized test scores. Applicants from an underrepresented minority group or from a predominantly minority high school can receive 20 points, as can children from low-income families—but only a maximum of 12 points for a perfect 1600 SAT result. Obviously, pigmentation counts for more than smarts in this calculus—is that, I wonder, what the late Justice Lewis Powell had in mind when he came up with the notion of "heightened judicial solicitude"? It is hardly surprising that a majority of Americans supports the Bush administration's decision to oppose the University of Michigan's admissions policies (Schmidt 2003). As Armstrong Williams, an African American strongly opposed to admissions policies that discriminate on the basis of race, notes, "a perfect SAT score is worth 12 points. Being black gets you 20 points. Is there anyone who can look at these two numbers and think they are fair? . . . That is why it pains me to see my peers rest their heads upon the warm pillow of victim status" (2003, 33). The university's law school does not use a points system but aims at achieving a "critical mass" of minority students. This, too, is highly problematic, as Justice Antonin Scalia observed in open court, "Once you use the term 'critical mass' you're into quota land."

Armstrong Williams is by no means the lone opposition; U.S. Secretary of Education (and Indiana University alumnus) Roderick Page is also unequivocal in his condemnation of the Michigan approach: "It is not right to fight discrimination with discrimination." See http://www.ed.gov/PressReleases/01–2003/01242003 .html. Most recently he ruffled a few feathers at the 2003 annual meeting of the Hispanic Association of Colleges and Universities by pointing out, quite reasonably, that "admissions quotas and double standards are not the answer," and that focusing more on elementary and secondary education would increase the possibility of applicants getting into college. Why this last point is not universally acknowledged beats me. Instead of tinkering with the apex of the education system, we should get to the root of the problem. This view has been espoused bluntly by Abigail Thernstrom (2003, A26), a Republican member of the U.S. Commission on Civil Rights: "We're playing little games to allow us to ignore the appalling racial gap in achievement in elementary schools, and this just continues to get these schools off the hook. . . . These plans compound a moral problem that Americans should be up in arms about."

Shelby Steele, also African American, provides an incisive dissection of white guilt before concluding, as anyone committed to nondiscriminatory practices must, that "there are, in fact, no races that need help: only individuals, citizens" (2003, 9). Even if one were persuaded that racial preferences were in principle a good thing, there are myriad practical problems associated with the implementation of affirmative action policies. Since income and social class are closely associated with educational performance and attainment (Renner 2003, 40), why wouldn't we, using a similar argument, weight the admissions process in favor of those, irrespective of race, who come from socially marginalized backgrounds? This point has been made tellingly by Curt Levy of the Center for Individual Rights: "It just doesn't make sense to give preference to the children of a wealthy black businessman but not the child of a Vietnamese boat person or an Arab-American who is suffering discrimination" (quoted here from Kantrowitz and Wingert 2003, 31). No matter how it is framed or sugarcoated, the University of Michigan admissions procedure is an instance of reverse discrimination. Whether the Supreme Court justices in their collective wisdom feel that it is inherently unconstitutional remains to be seen.

And now for a local illustration of zaniness in pursuit of the holy grail of soi-disant diversity: The IU Bloomington campus boasts a number of murals by the independently minded American realist painter Thomas Hart Benton (a teacher of Jackson Pollock). One mural in particular, *Parks, the Circus, the Klan, the Press*, has had a checkered life since its unveiling in the Hoosier state back in the 1930s. The problem (for some) is that this mural, currently located in a classroom, includes a depiction of the Ku Klux Klan. Over the years, controversy has occasionally flared up among sections of the black student body, who find that the KKK imagery constitutes, in the phraseology of the moment, a "hostile climate" (for some context and historical background, see www.indiana.edu/~deanfac/benton/). The Benton issue burst open again in 2002, with some students calling for the mural's removal. After much high-profile debate and discussion across campus, our recently installed chancellor made a Solomon-like decision: the mural would stay in place, but a diversity education program would be built around Benton's offending work.

Educational sessions now follow a nine-minute video about Benton's artwork, and students are given cards on which to write their personal reactions to the mural. After these sessions, if students still feel that the climate is hostile, they are encouraged to discuss the matter with a faculty member, and, if that is still not adequate, they may contact the euphoniously named IU Bloomington Racial Incidents Team in their sad quest for closure. Ah, there I've uttered it, "that ghastly word *closure*"! (Vidal 2002, 92). The good thing is that (for now) the mural has not been removed or covered up; the bad news is that IU (a leading research university, no less) has exhibited a form of intellectual pusillanimity utterly at odds with its scholarly pedigree and its lustrous history of supporting freedom of thought and expression—Indiana University, after all, was home to Alfred Kinsey, whose pioneering studies of human sexuality are still too much for some of the Hoosier natives. And, as if all that weren't enough, we also have the prospect of an annual lecture entitled "State of Diversity" delivered by the chancellor. The IU solution is infantilizing; another example of how efforts at affirmative action and/or diversity are counterproductive.

I grew up in a country where dark deeds have been perpetrated for centuries by one group or another, deeds that have often been recorded in paintings, sculptures, literature, music, and song. The history of Ireland includes representations that, inevitably, conjure up searing memories for one side or the other. For centuries, limited civil rights were granted to the Catholic population of Northern Ireland, but no one has ever suggested that these historic injustices can be undone, or atoned for, by expunging or sugarcoating elements of the country's Protestant artistic and cultural heritage. Ireland, as with so many nations, has its Benton murals—as a quick sightseeing tour of Belfast will make abundantly clear—but we can, just about, live with them. History, however painful, needs to be taught, not sanitized and rewritten. And where better to do that than at a research university?

Historical airbrushing is an extraordinarily dangerous path to travel: Where does one draw the line? Who draws the line? Should the line be permanent? If the Benton murals are to be secreted away to avoid offense, should the curtain also come down over Picasso's *Guernica*? Should *Mein Kampf* be removed from the shelves? Should Wagner's music not be performed in Israel? It's a short and slippery slope from banning Benton in Bloomington to blasting Buddhas in Afghanistan.

REFERENCES

Kantrowitz, B., and P. Wingert. 2003. "What's at Stake?" *Newsweek* (January 27): 30–37.

Mangan, K. S. 2003. "Indiana U. Law School Defends Affirmative Action after a Recent Graduate Raises Complaints." *Chronicle of Higher Education.* chronicle.com/daily/2003/05/2003052703n.htm [accessed May 27, 2003].

Renner, K. E. 2003. "Racial Equality and Higher Education." *Academe* (January–February): 38–43.

Rothman, S. 2003. "Is Diversity Overrated?" *New York Times* (March 29): A11.

Schmidt, P. 2003. "Poll Finds Wide Support for Bush's Stance Against Michigan's Race-Conscious Admissions Policies." *Chronicle of Higher Education.* chronicle.com/daily/2003/02/2003020701n.htm [accessed April 2, 2003].

Steele, S. 2003. "Black Doubts in an Age of White Guilt." *Sunday Times* (January 19): 9 (section 5).

Thernstrom, A. 2003. Quoted here from S. Hebel, "'Percent Plans' Don't Add Up." *Chronicle of Higher Education* (March 21): A22–24, A26.

Vidal, G. 2002. *Perpetual War for Perpetual Peace: How We Got to Be So Hated.* New York: Thunder's Mouth Press.

Williams, A. 2003. "Diversity Is Essential . . . But Not at This Cost." *Newsweek* (January 27): 33.

CAN YOU "CELEBRATE" DIVERSITY?

Originally published September 2003

We celebrate birthdays, sporting victories, jubilees. One does not celebrate diversity. To do so is to misuse language. "Celebrate diversity!" is a vacuous exhortation, yet it has become the rallying cry of a depressing number of muddled, though presumably well-meaning, participants at academic and professional conferences across the nation.

Google generated 320,000 hits when I entered the term "workplace diversity," and 16,500 for "celebrate diversity." That tells you something straight away. Today, there is a veritable army of diversity trainers and counselors making a living by peddling their snake oil to clients, ranging from Fortune 500 companies to humble library systems. The language of this mini-industry is itself an eye-opener: We have "Admissions Diversity Counselor," "Diversity Coordinator" (How, pray, does one coordinate diversity?), "Diversity Counselor," "Cultural Diversity Counselor," and even "Certified Diversity Counselor." And that is before we throw "multicultural" and "ethnic" into the lexical stew.

Only the other day I stumbled across something on the IU Bloomington campus called the Commission on Multicultural Understanding (COMU). COMU, I'm thrilled to discover, has a Diversity Training Committee and provides diversity facilitation. And our nation's campus bureaucrats are no slouches when it comes to crafting policies with Monty Pythonesque titles. Take this example of the genre from California Polytechnic State University in San

7

Luis Obispo: "Resolution to Enhance Civility and Promote a Diversity-Friendly Campus Climate" (O'Neil 2003). It's as if merely approving some half-witted resolutions could thermostatically regulate the mood or spirit of a campus. To make matters worse, these constructs and terminology are reminiscent of totalitarian regimes. As Diane Ravitch has observed: "Only a George Orwell could fully appreciate how honorable words like *fairness* and *diversity* have been deployed to impose censorship and uniformity on everyday language" (2003, 80). Or, to provide a contemporary perspective, you might spend a few minutes leafing through the sensitivity and bias guidelines used routinely by educational publishers, such as the following exemplar: "Reflecting Diversity: Multicultural Guidelines for Educational Publishing Professionals," produced by McGraw-Hill (Ravitch 2003, 41–46).

The rot has spread to Libraryland. I read recently that the Online Community Library Center (OCLC), the bibliographic utility, has used the services of the intriguingly named Global Lead Management Corporation, a consulting firm that specializes in diversity and inclusion issues in the workplace, to educate its staff about culturally based communications behaviors. No doubt, some of you have had firsthand experience with diversity training or sensitivity workshops, and, no doubt, many will e-mail me indignantly to let me know how useful these events were. But quaffable snake oil is still snake oil.

People are different; the differences between groups and individuals are many and complex and cannot be reduced to a handful of politically correct categories based primarily on pigmentation. Using a couple of personal examples, I will illustrate why I have a problem with the totalizing rhetoric of diversity. Several years ago an administrator at Indiana University (blessedly since departed) told me that he would like to take the academic deans (overwhelmingly male and white at the time) to a basketball game attended largely by African Americans so that we could experience firsthand what it was like to be in a minority. It was a lamentably naïve and patronizing suggestion. I didn't bother pointing out to my colleague that I had been at events and in places all over the globe where I was the only Caucasian to be seen and that I might, just occasionally, have engaged in a little critical reflexivity as a result.

During a recent interview at an East Coast institution, I was asked about my views on "diversity." Naturally, I said that I was all for diversity, broadly understood. However, I added that it seemed to me as if the term carried certain local (i.e., truncated) connota-, tions—which it does. "Diversity" at this nameless campus was code for African American and/or Hispanic. I tried to point out that such a working definition lacked—how shall I put it?— inclusivity, but I was quickly put in my place. Diversity is the new orthodoxy on campus, and, as Bruce Thornton has observed, "public obeisance to it is necessary for the ambitious" (2001, 3). Such, dear reader, is the realpolitik of campus life. I have witnessed it repeatedly firsthand as otherwise intelligent colleagues, both professors and administrators, have been reduced to parroting the incoherent mantras of multiculturalism and diversity, fearful of deviating from the prevailing orthodoxy. Certain group identities matter; others do not. That fact, naturally, remains largely unspoken. As for individual identities, forget it! Kors and Silvergate made this point tellingly and succinctly in their fine book *The Shadow University*: "Universities operate with a humanly impoverished notion of 'diversity,' excluding personality, social class, spirituality, taste and private passions" (1998, 193).

Does my pale skin necessarily make me more or less like a dark-skinned peer than any one, or all, of the other factors listed above by Kors and Silvergate? Frankly, I have my doubts—which isn't to deny the importance of group variables such as culture or language. But I, for one, find it demeaning to be reduced to a single category—one, moreover, that focuses on external attributes to the exclusion of all else.

Apparently, I am not alone in having some misgivings about this "simplistic racialist view of culture" (Thornton 2001, 9) and the way in which the concept of diversity is being mobilized within academia, the library profession, and all points beyond. In one of his *American Libraries* editorials, Leonard Kniffel, to his credit, asked a simple but sensible question: "What does 'diversity' include? Everybody but heterosexual white men and a few 'powerful' white women?" (2002, 460). As a member of the former group—now a bona fide minority—I would like to know why we, too, cannot have a piece of the great diversity pie just like everybody else. Are we, to appropriate the reasoning of Bertrand Russell, members of a class that is not a member of itself?

We are all so busy slicing and dicing ourselves into ever-smaller groups that the ties that bind are fraying. If I may paraphrase John Donne, "No minority is an island, entire of itself." Yet, multicultural (and other) special interest groups are proliferating at a disconcerting rate, fragmenting the whole and creating increasingly balkanized discourse communities as the mania for identity politics takes root. We are building, unwittingly, a Tower of Babel in the name of diversity, and it will serve us ill in the long run—hardly grounds for celebration.

REFERENCES

Kniffel, L. 2002. Editorial, *American Libraries* (June/July): 460.

Kors, A. C., and H. A. Sivergate. 1998. *The Shadow University: The Betrayal of Liberty on America's Campuses.* New York: Free Press.

O'Neil, R. 2003. "What Limits Should Campus Networks Place on Pornography?" *Chronicle of Higher Education* (March 21): B20.

Ravitch, D. 2003. *The Language Police: How Pressure Groups Restrict What Students Learn.* New York: Knopf.

Thornton, B. 2001. "Cultivating Sophistry." Pp. 3–27 in *Bonfire of the Humanities: Rescuing the Classics in an Impoverished Age*, V. D. Hanson, J. Heath, and B. S. Thornton. Wilmington, Del.: ISI Books.

"HE MAY BE RETRO BUT [HE'S] NOT DONE SPEWING"

The "he" in the title refers to me. This memorable phrase was the subject line of a January 2003 e-mail post by the University Librarian of the University of California, Santa Barbara, on FEMINIST, the American Library Association's (ALA) Feminist Task Force Discussion List. In *Pulp Friction* (Cronin 2003), I offer the reader a sampling of the exothermic, locker-room language favored by some of FEMINIST's subscribers, and it would be remiss of me not to provide an update to devotees of this subgenre of feminist discourse.

But first, some context. In January 2003 I announced that I would be demitting office as dean of the Indiana University School of Library and Information Science (SLIS) six months hence. This less-than-earth-shattering announcement prompted one Diedre Conkling to post the following message: "Considering the earlier comments made on this list about Blaise Cronin this announcement may spark a bit of joy." Naturally, I could not resist pinging an e-mail (privately, I hasten to add) to Ms. Conkling to say that I was happy to be able to ignite some joy in the most unlikely of places. I also recommended that she read the just-published *Pulp Friction*.

This fairly innocuous communication triggered instantaneous shock waves. First, it meant that I was either a pseudonymous subscriber to FEMINIST ("Could he be a closet member under an assumed name?" asked Lynne Ingersoll), or, perish the thought, there was a mole (or moles) on the listserv funneling messages to

11

me. Ms. Conkling was quickly joined by Kathleen de la Peña Mc-Cook who, never one to mince words, referred to me as "Library-land's greatest woman-despiser . . . a tumid know-it-all who has no ideas and is happiest belittling others." But my favorite, since we're on the subject of contumely, was another gem again from the splenetic Ms. McCook, a distinguished university professor at the University of South Florida no less, who labeled me a "retro-boob." This would be funny if it weren't so unwittingly ironic. But let's move on to the more substantive issues, which this little spat provoked.

First, the fact that I had access to discussions on FEMINIST seems to have caused a few souls a degree of angst; Theresa Tobin wrote: "I will put the suggestion of a closed list on the Feminist Task Force Agenda as part of the usual report on the listserv," though to her credit she did "not support the idea." I could well understand this sort of reaction if I were trolling or harassing indi-vidual subscribers, but that was not the case. Susan Kane was sen-sible and pragmatic: "Not to be obnoxious, but no one should ex-pect anything that they post to a newsgroup to be private unless they were specifically promised that privacy." I find it most pecu-liar that a group of librarians, representative of a profession pur-portedly committed to transparency and openness, would want to restrict access to information. If individuals wish to gossip pri-vately, they can, of course, create an appropriate mechanism, but an ALA-sponsored listserv is hardly such a forum.

Second, member reaction to *Pulp Friction*'s publication was most revealing. Ms. Pritchard posted: "In fact, and I am appalled, a collection of his essays has just been issued by Scarecrow Press, sponsors of the ALA Equality Award. When I saw this I wrote to their acquisitions editor . . . and complained. Personally I am not sure what I will do but it is upsetting to see one of my long-time favorite presses, one that has consistently supported serious work on women's issues, endorse the writings of Blaise Cronin." It's one thing to diss my writings, but it's quite another to try to influence a press—one with whom I first published in 1991, as it happens (Cronin and Davenport 1991)—regarding its publication policies. (Full marks to my editor, Sue Easun, and Scarecrow Press for re-sisting such shameful bullying tactics.) Is this not the very kind of censorious practice to which the ALA is implacably opposed? But Ms. Pritchard did not stop there. As debate swirled around possi-ble reviewers for *Pulp Friction*, she posted the following message to the list: "I'd love to review this book but I'm sure I cannot ethi-cally do so since I'm slammed in one of Blaise's little diatribes. Please, some good person out there—with a strong stomach and a highly analytical mind to dissect his silly philosophies—take this on!"

It is hardly cause for concern that a few colleagues get a buzz from slinging insults electronically, but there should be collective concern that the actions of some leaders in the profession vary pro-foundly with the norms and values they so vehemently assert in public. In fairness I ought to point out that this is neither a new nor a peculiarly online phenomenon. Twelve years ago, when I came to the United States to take up the deanship at Indiana Uni-versity, I was greeted in the professional press (e.g., *Library Jour-nal, Wilson Library Bulletin*) with a barrage of perplexingly per-sonal comments by individuals whom I had never met: "Brain drain refugee"; "Import who offers dim hope that he truly under-stands us"; and "Unlikely that he will offer much intelligent direc-tion to Indiana"—all fine examples of what has been termed "hon-est nativism and xenophobia in the good old-fashioned, paranoid American style" (Hanson 2001, 119). Evidently, not much has changed over the years.

FEMINIST has proved an eye-opener for me, not simply in terms of the stridency and vulgarity of the language used by some subscribers, but also in the way these exchanges expose the disso-nance between public posture and private practice. But perhaps I should move on to other targets and leave the Feministas, in the words of Shakespeare, "chanting faint hymns to the cold fruitless moon" (*A Midsummer Night's Dream*, 1.1).

REFERENCES

Cronin, B. 2003. *Pulp Friction*. Lanham, Md.: Scarecrow Press.

Cronin, B., and E. Davenport. 1991. *Elements of Information Management*. Metuchen, N.J.: Scarecrow Press.

Hanson, V. D. 2001. "Too Much Ego in Your Cosmos." Pp. 93–135 in *Bonfire of the Humanities: Rescuing the Classics in an Impoverished Age*, V. D. Hanson, J. Heath, and B. S. Thornton. Wilmington, Del.: ISI Books.

Mollycoddling Mediocrities

"Men must be taught as if you taught them not."

—Alexander Pope

The customer is not always right—at least not in higher education, where use of the term *customer* for *student* has become widely accepted. Students may pay their way, but that does not mean that they know what is good for them. Call me an unreconstructed fogey, but the title of (full) professor, traditionally understood, means that one, in fact, professes. In Britain it is still the assumption (certainly in older universities) that when one is appointed to a chair (in philosophy, mathematics, or whatever) one speaks ex cathedra, that is to say, with earned authority and with demonstrable knowledge of one's field.

Young and (sometimes) not so young minds attend universities to learn (when they're not binge drinking, that is). They learn primarily from their professors, the anointed experts in a given domain. This relationship is most simply, if unfashionably, characterized as that of master and apprentice and ideally enacted in weekly tutorials. For good or ill, the sage on the stage is increasingly giving way to the guide on the side, though there are some who still acknowledge that the best teaching "doesn't always happen around a seminar table" (Bartlett 2003, A12). It is rather different from the relationship between a customer and, say, a storeowner or parking valet. But such a characterization is, apparently, anathema to many. Students increasingly see themselves as customers buying chunks of education, just as they buy DVDs or groceries, and are encouraged in this self-delusion by the complicit actions of administrators. Students seem to know what they want and need, and, thus, should be provided with a syllabus that is just to their liking and a teaching style that makes them feel "respected as an individual."

Every semester for the past twelve years I have read every student evaluation for all of my full-time faculty—that means literally hundreds of survey forms. I should point out that the instrument we use (the survey form) has about as much construct validity as a roll of toilet paper and that the battery of questions constituting the survey instrument is designed to solicit students' likes and dislikes, rather than to determine what has laughingly become known as the "quality of the educational experience" or "learning outcomes." The process has been described justly by one of my colleagues as a "product satisfaction survey." There are good teachers, bad teachers, and some great teachers. We know who they are, and they probably know themselves. Whenever I read such banalities as "Professor X is hot," "Professor Y's reading list is too long," or "Professor Z did not give me enough eye contact," I am not sure whether to laugh or cry. But at least I'm not a lone wolf howling at the lunacy of the situation. Harvey Mansfield (2003, 18), reflecting on his many years at Harvard, excoriates the limitations of the customer-centric (*sic*) model of higher education:

> Course evaluations by students . . . undermine the authority of professors. They make professors accountable to students on the basis of needing to please them, like businesses pleasing customers or elected officials pleasing voters. The superiority of those who know over those who don't is slighted, and the students' judgment comes down to the charm of the professor as students perceive it. What at first might be justified as useful feedback from students ends up distorting the relationship between professors and students.

The fetishization of course evaluations, and the prominent role they have been granted in faculty reviews and salary setting exercises, have had a corrosive effect on both faculty morale and academic standards. Student evaluations have become tools for demeaning professors and dumbing down the classroom experience. They give voice to those whose voices should be relatively muted in such matters. The myopia, pettiness, vindictiveness, and sarcasm all too often revealed in student evaluations testify to how misguided the exercise has become. Recent developments in the creation of Web-based faculty rating schemes (e.g., ratemyprofessors.com) will merely exacerbate this lamentable trend. Predictably, those students most likely to post comments are those who have something negative or ad hominem to say. I have examined some of these online sites and am appalled at the selectivity and spitefulness of what is publicly accessible. No wonder some professors have resorted to litigation in an effort to protect their reputations. The lunatics are running the asylum.

You know the old saw: those who can, do; those who can't, teach. In academia, the riff runs as follows: those who can, teach; those who can't, administer. As the administrator population grows much faster than that of the full-time faculty, busywork needs to be found for the sprawling ranks of assistant, associate, and vice-this-that-and-the-other. What better way than by creating a mini-bureaucracy devoted to classroom civility as a way to soak up the surplus labor?

I was a student for more than a few years, and I've also taught for many years on both sides of the Atlantic and in many other countries around the globe, but I have never felt a need to consult or invoke a so-called civility code. Since this may all be new to you, let me provide a little clarification. Apparently, our discriminating customers have the idea that a classroom is a cross between a playground and a cafeteria. Moreover, they seem to feel that since they help pay the professor's mortgage, they should also determine what kinds of behaviors will be tolerated in the classroom. Instead of simply booting these unruly elements out of the classroom, giving them a failing grade, or rusticating them, the system, in its wisdom, has come up with a "super wheeze," one designed to ensure that more administrative posts are created without, at the same time, entirely alienating our cherished customers. This is where civility codes come in. These are sometimes discussed under the rubric of campus climate. I'll spare you the many vogue definitions of campus climate for another day. Suffice it to say that there is a bibliography of campus climate reports hosted on the Web by the National Consortium of Directors of LGBT (Lesbian, Gay, Bisexual, and Transgender) Resources in Higher Education (www.lgbt campus.org/resources/campus_climate.html), should you feel the need for some immediate self-education.

I checked a few of these so-called civility codes (take a look at the "Guidelines for Classroom Civility and Respect" posted on the Web by the University of Massachusetts, Amherst, for a flavor of the genre) and was suitably deflated. For instance, the syllabus for a computing course at a university in North Carolina included the following guidelines: "Turn off your cell phone before class starts. . . . Don't read the newspaper during class. . . . Don't listen to electronic or audio equipment during class. . . . No prolonged conversations during class." Why, I wondered, would anyone want to do any of the above while attending class? One knows how to behave in class, and, if one doesn't, one shouldn't be attending class in the first place. If university administrators hadn't been so diffident about reading the riot act in recent years and were less concerned with placating their narcissistic customers, we would never have reached this point. Make students accept responsibility for their own actions or face the consequences, and to hell with the idiocies of climate management. Leave that to the heating engineers.

REFERENCES

Bartlett, T. 2003. "Big But Not Bad." *Chronicle of Higher Education* (May 9): A12–A14.

Mansfield, H. C. 2002. "Acceptance Address: Harvard's Virtue." *Academic Questions* 15, no. 4:15–20.

SARTORIAL SHENANIGANS

Times and fashions have changed. As a freshman at Trinity College, Dublin, I was required to wear a gown on certain occasions. My knee-length black robe flowed in the breeze as I scuttled across Front Square to the Public Theatre or Dining Hall. Today, robed undergraduates are an anachronism, though the term *gown* retains its metonymic potency: one has only to think of that habitually invoked phrase "town and gown."

Colorful robes and exotic headdress (from fez and bonnet to pill box and mortar board) still feature prominently in academic life, accompanied (not always, it must be said) by the appropriate subfusc clothing. At the risk of stating the obvious, Bermuda shorts and T-shirts should not be worn with academic robes, nor should balloons be affixed to mortar boards. In case you did not know, the Burgon Society exists to promote the study of academic dress (www.burgon.org.uk/index.html). For events such as Founder's Day or the university's semiannual commencement ceremonies, I have two splendid sets of full robes (scarlet and royal blue) with bell-shaped sleeves, hoods, and soft, tasseled bonnets upon which to call. This mode of attire has considerable pedigree, going back to medieval times. The ancient universities of Coimbra (Portugal) and Oxford (England) were among the first to prescribe certain kinds of academic regalia, and to this day the traditions of academic apparel are (in the main) adhered to rigorously, although there are no universal rules as such.

In his introduction to *Academic Dress of the University of Oxford* (Venables and Clifford 1998, 1), Sir Richard Southwood notes that academic dress "is an outward sign of the universality of universities; of their responsibility for certain timeless values essential to the freedom of enquiry: tolerance of alternative views and courage in maintaining one's own, tirelessness in the pursuit of truth and the free exchange of knowledge." Sadly, some of one's peers seem to have lost sight of the symbolism, as they mindlessly craft unconstitutional speech codes, neuter robust debate, and impose ludicrous quotas of one kind or another across the nation's campuses. Perhaps these "fashionistas" of the New Age university should wear their gowns a little more often.

In this country, there are, I was recently pleased to discover, explicit guidelines pertaining to the wearing of academic garb. Eugene Sullivan of the American Council on Education (ACE) is the author of "An Academic Costume Code and An Academic Ceremony Guide" (1997) a document that specifies what should be worn, when, how, and by whom. Over the years, the ACE's Committee on Academic Costumes and Ceremonies has periodically reviewed the costume code and made a number of modest changes. On the key issue, though, Sullivan is adamant: "The governing force is tradition and the continuity of academic symbols from the Middle Ages. The tradition should be departed from as little as possible." The recommendation relating to subfusc dress is no less explicit: "Shoes and other articles of visible apparel worn by graduates should be of dark colors that harmonize with the academic costume. Nothing else should be worn on the academic gown." It was the last sentence that particularly caught my attention. This means that one cannot, for example, attach a sprig of shamrock to one's gown in order to flag one's Irishness, nor affix a lapel pin to show one support for the Republican Party. Make one exception to this rule, and we are off down the slippery slope of unbridled self-expression. Academic attire combines history, symbolism, and gravitas: it is not a matter of personal style or preference. At least it was not until recently.

Two years ago, our current chancellor appeared in the robing room with what I believe is called a Kente stole or sash (typically made from West African handwoven material) draped over her academic robes. (For the record, she is Caucasian and a graduate of America's oldest university.) This was not altogether novel: in recent years, some African American students have taken to adorning themselves with similar accoutrements at their graduation ceremonies. But it is something else for a senior administrator to break with tradition in this manner, and it is disturbing on a number of counts. First, it shows an ignorance of, if not disdain toward, the conventions of academic dress and ritual. Second, it reveals the spinelessness of university administrators and trustees when it comes to enforcing codified standards. Third, it sets an unfortunate precedent. If one group decides to differentiate itself via ethnic, political, or ideological signifiers, what is to stop other minorities (or mainstream groups, for that matter) from following suit? One can imagine a situation where graduation ceremonies across the nation become little more than jamborees to make sartorially inspired statements (social or personal) by individuals from whom we should expect more savoir faire. The action of our chancellor is regrettable insofar as it shows scant regard for the venerable traditions of both an institution and a system that predate her by eight centuries and will likely outlive her by many more. Empty gestures of this kind really have no place at solemn academic ceremonies.

I may be in a minority on this issue, but I'm pleased to say that I am not a lone voice in the wilderness of political incorrectness. Recently, a federal judge ruled that school officials in Denver had the right to ban all adornments from graduation attire, which put the kibosh on the plans of black seniors to wear multicolored Kente cloths over their graduation gowns. Bonnets and mortar boards off to the right-thinking principal of Arvada High School for sticking to his sartorial guns! And there is some historical precedent, according to the University of Kent website: "A decree from the University of Paris in 1339 suggests that masters and doctors were turning up to faculty meetings in flamboyant mantles and 'sleeveless tunics.' The decree threatens these casually dressed luminaries with the loss of their vote at meetings and with suspension from teaching for a whole year if they refused to leave the meeting when asked to do so" (www.kent.ac.uk/about/tradition/dress.html). If the dastardly French could do it in the fourteenth century, it is surely now time for U.S. higher education to bite the sartorial bullet.

REFERENCES

Sullivan, E. 1997. *An Academic Costume Code and an Academic Ceremony Guide*. Reprinted with permission from *American Universities and Colleges*. Walter de Gruyter, Inc. www.acenet.edu/faq/costume_code.html [accessed May 18, 2003].

Venables, D. R., and R. E. Clifford. 1998. *Academic Dress of the University of Oxford*. Oxford: J. & P. Venables.

Rites and Wrongs of Passage

Once upon a time I was a schoolboy. There were teachers and pupils (from the Latin *pupillus*, male ward) in a school, located on school grounds. Later I went to university, where I mixed with fellow students on campus. I graduated from university and embarked on an academic career, an aspiring scholar. Pupil, student, scholar. Life was simple, language clear. No more.

My daughter, in high school, is a student (not a pupil) on a campus (not school grounds) taught by a faculty (not schoolteachers). She will happily attend something ghastly called a prom and "graduate" from high school, because that, apparently, is what one does. Actually, it is what one does at middle and junior high schools, too, as far as I can tell. Predictably, I don't get it.

Schools have dictionaries. Why don't administrators or—to use an abominable neologism—educators, use them more often? A pupil is not a student is not a scholar. It's all so achingly pretentious and, ultimately, socially damaging. Schools do not need to appropriate the terminology of universities and colleges, nor should they ape their rituals (see "Sartorial Shenanigans" in this volume); rather, they should develop their own protocols. Schools are schools—places where children are taught and learn. School*children* are just that. Why deny them their childhood? Why inflate their status? Why accelerate them into adulthood? The rituals and attire of graduation have evolved over the centuries and are an important element of university life. They have no place in the school system. Imitation may be the sincerest form of flattery, but what's happening in the nation's primary and secondary schools is also, I sense, part of a broader, deeply disconcerting trend.

Dressing our pimply progeny in tuxedos and ball gowns, sending them off to proms in hideous stretch limousines, and wrapping them in plastic graduation robes, naturally makes one think of six-year-old JonBenet Ramsey and the meretricious world of "Little Miss" beauty pageants. This child's murder cast the spotlight on a penumbral world populated by young girls strutting their stuff on stage, wannabe Marilyns or Madonnas, egged on by their seriously misguided and single-minded parents. The language used by the media to describe JonBenet was appropriately and unreservedly condemnatory: "a painted baby, a sexualized toddler beauty queen." See www.crimelibrary.com/ramseymain.htm. It is a mystery to me why parents encourage this cruel loss of innocence; equally, I am perplexed that this society, at once so enlightened and puritanical, can tolerate such unabashed sexualization of minors.

But perhaps I shouldn't be surprised, given how the nation's school system has apparently embarked on a misguided mission to eradicate childhood and all the symbolic accoutrements thereof. Mimicking adults seems to be the goal of the current generation of "educrats" (Thornton 2001, 5), armed with their dubious doctorates of Education and Philosophy from equally dubious schools of education. Make our kids think they are grown-ups long before their minds and bodies have matured, and be damned. Perhaps if we dress them like adults and label them adults, they'll behave like adults. Well, it works: remember Columbine?

REFERENCE

Thornton, B. "Cultivating Sophistry." Pp. 3–27 in *Bonfire of the Humanities: Rescuing the Classics in an Impoverished* Age, V. D. Hanson, J. Heath, and B. S. Thornton. Wilmington, Del.: ISI Books.

DISRUPTIVE TECHNOLOGIES

Most business books should be pulped at birth. The distinguishing characteristics of the genre are gaudiness, vacuity, and faddishness in more or less equal measure. And daft titles: I recently saw one in Borders entitled *Primal Leadership* (Goleman, McKee, and Boyatzis, 2002). Bulging with nostrums and perky phraseology, many of these short-lived business bestsellers are noticeably thin on empirical data. But every so often an original work appears on the publishing scene and makes a serious and well-deserved splash. Michael Porter's blockbusters on competitive strategy and competitive advantage helped make the Harvard professor a virtual brand name—a true academic megastar (see www.ics. hbs.edu). A more recent example is Clayton Christensen (also from the Harvard B-school stable), whose *Innovator's Dilemma* (2000) has proved to be something of hit with both academics and practitioners.

Not all of what Christensen has to say is new; other tomes have explored S-curves, product life cycles, technological innovation, diffusion rates, and zones of discontinuity, and there is a considerable literature on media substitution theory, but what Christensen has done is marshal loads of empirical data from a variety of industrial and service sectors (e.g., disk drives, accounting software, steel, automobiles) to support his theory of why successful firms sometimes falter. He chronicles the number of companies that have engaged in "sustaining innovation," adding, in other words, more and more layers of sophistication or feature-richness to a product for an important and established customer segment. The net effect is what he terms "performance oversupply," or functionality fetishism, if you wish. One consequence is that those who lack the financial means or skills to benefit from a particular product or service are effectively locked out of the market. In Type-I disruptions, a competitor launches a product that is comparatively simple and/or cheaper to use and thus of potentially broad appeal. The innovator in this case is providing the market with a novel product; examples he cites are PCs, the telephone, and personal financial management software. Each of these technological innovations created a new market: for those who could not access mainframes; for those who could use/get to the telegraph office; and for those who could not afford tax consultants. Type-II disruptions, on the other hand, occur when a supplier or manufacturer targets the soft underbelly, or low end, of the existing market with an appealing alternative to the prevailing model. Examples of this are discount retailing, steel mini-mills, and no-frills airlines. Over time, the once-dominant players begin to see their market share diminish and their customers migrate to the products of interlopers.

When I read the first edition of Christensen's book in 1997 (a year in which I was, additionally, appointed director of distance education at Indiana University), I quickly thought about the implications of his ideas for my world—the fairly conservative world of higher education. Universities have become more and more expensive, making access a near-impossibility for many who lack the financial resources, time, or grades to gain admission—not to mention those who are geographically disenfranchised. They typically offer multiyear degree programs rather than personalized skills modules or workplace-relevant training at a time when retooling is in ever greater demand (Cronin 1998). A simplistic reading of Christensen might suggest that universities have been too busy sustaining innovation in a very traditional and largely residential model (more of the same and better) to take cognizance of wider societal changes and the shifting needs of the labor force. Since then, he has considered the potentially disruptive effects of, for instance, corporate training and the emergence of distributed education and online distance providers (such as the hugely successful University of Phoenix) on traditional models of business and management education www.educause.edu/ir/library/pdf/ffpiu013.pdf). The new breed of cyberuniversity and corporate training provider targets those who (1) have previously been nonconsumers, (2) will be happy with a relatively simple or stripped-down product, and (3) can do what they want more easily with the new product (e.g., solve problems and gain qualifications that will earn promotion).

A while ago, I read an interview with Christensen in which he was asked the following question: "Is the Internet disrupting your own business?" Here's what he had to say (www.businessweek.com/cgi-bin/ebiz/ebiz_frame.pl?url = /ebiz/9903/315clay.htm): "I worry a lot about the Harvard Business School. Our business model and our products have become very expensive. They're the highest-performing products in management education. But coming at the bottom are online courses, which can't today appeal to the mainstream of our customers." Harvard is, of course, as blue chip as it gets and, at the upper end of the market demand, is unlikely to evaporate. Yet, as Christensen recognizes, even the strongest brands (top-ranking Ivy League B-schools) will have to diversify their products and delivery platforms if they are to retain their leadership positions in the increasingly diverse higher education marketplace.

In any event, I don't expect Harvard's MBA program to go belly-up anytime soon (the power of the Cambridge brand name and the associated cachet are well nigh impossible to match), but what about the generic MLS degree? Are there new entrants and substitute products waiting in the wings? Couldn't Phoenix or some other provider muscle into the library science market with an attractive suite of online offerings, modules targeted at particular segments of the marketplace and designed to transfer skills that would be of real practical value? Since time immemorial, we have heard practitioners cri icize library schools for their excessive emphasis on theory and abstractions, irrelevant curricula, and graduates' lack of practical know-how (e.g., Cronin 1982). If Christensen's thinking is correct, then we might expect to see sub-master's level programs and certificates coming onstream, just as less-expensive associate degree programs have, he claims, become the major supply route for qualified nurses (rather than the more academic four-year degree programs) without any appreciable difference in the quality of the clinical training.

For an equivalent shift to occur in Libraryland, we'd need to relax, if not remove, the cumbersome and arcane accreditation standards that are currently in place. And, while I'm on the subject, let me point out that the ALA has recently launched a companion organization, the Allied Professional Association (APA), a bureaucratic carbuncle par excellence, designed to deal with the certification of individuals. Talk about over-egging the custard. In many regards, both professional and paraprofessional librarians would benefit from the kind of cheap and accessible education and training alternatives that Christensen connotes with the phrase "disruptive technologies." New modes of provision and new forms of training modules would find, I imagine, a highly receptive market and would be of inestimable practical value to those who work at the coalface. There'd still be room for a few good graduate programs, of course, but some of the weaker schools would go by the board. Such a liberation of the education and training marketplace in Libraryland could quite easily be achieved, but first we need to get rid of the suffocating paraphernalia of accreditation and certification, two processes that merely create bureaucratic bloat and drag.

REFERENCES

Christensen, C. M. 2000. *The Innovator's Dilemma: When New Technologies Cause Great Firms to Fail*. Cambridge, Mass.: Harvard Business School Press, 2000.

Cronin, B. 1982. *The Education of Library-Information Professionals: A Conflict of Objectives?* London: Aslib.

————. 1998. "The Electronic Academy Revisited." *Aslib Proceedings* 50, no. 9:241–54.

Goleman, D., McKee, A., and Boyatzis, R.E. 2002. *Primal Leadership: Realizing the Power of Emotional Intelligence.* Cambridge, Mass.: Harvard Business School Press.

Very Well Endowed

Last Saturday, the phone rang in my office. It was a young lady from Trinity College, Dublin demurely enquiring if I were interested, in principle, in staying in touch with my alma mater and, who knows, perhaps making a terribly modest donation at some point in the future. A pleasant (if rather unfocused) exchange ensued, and no promises were made. I graduated more than thirty years ago, yet this is the first time I have been approached directly. That, surely, could not have happened in this country. To date, I have not given a cent to Trinity, an institution that I hold in some affection. I have, on the other hand, given a few shekels to Indiana University. At first glance, this may seem odd, but it speaks to the relative sophistication of, and commitment to, fundraising on both sides of the Atlantic. By way of an aside, my U.K. colleagues find the idea of giving to one's employing institution nothing less than incomprehensible. What they would make of the fact that faculty at the Bloomington campus of Indiana University contributed something like $17 million or so during the last capital campaign, I cannot imagine.

The endowment numbers in this country are simply astounding. Harvard reported $17.1 billion this year, down from an all-time high of $19.2 billion in 2000 (Pulley 2003). But what's a couple of billion in this league? To put things in perspective, Harvard's endowment is greater than the gross domestic product of many sub-Saharan nations, and the earned interest on its endowment is more than the annual operating budget of many large U.S. universities. According to the latest data, about forty universities have endowments with a market value of $1 billion or above, and the aggregate endowment value of the twenty top-performing institutions is just over $100 billion, if my arithmetic is correct. Without these funds, most institutions would struggle to cover their operating expenses; some universities, in fact, rely on investment income generated by their endowments to cover as much as 40 percent of their operating budget (Pulley 2003, A26). And it's just not the privates that have impressive endowments; among the ranks of the nation's public institutions, the Texas and California systems have amassed multibillion-dollar endowments.

Nowhere else on earth does this scale of giving occur. In the United Kingdom, only the universities of Oxford and Cambridge can boast endowments that would seem impressive by American standards. In general, the campaign targets and results achieved by the rest are, to put it politely, nugatory. Not surprisingly, as the U.K. higher education system moves toward the American model, British universities are realizing that fundraising will soon be a sine qua non of successful functioning, as government support contracts. As a result we're seeing a steady stream of visitors coming here to pick our brains. But techniques (which even today are still a subtle admixture of art and science in this business) are only part of the picture, albeit an important one. Several of my colleagues at Indiana University recently coauthored a 600-page textbook on fundraising—sometimes referred to with the euphemism "institutional advancement"—which gives a detailed insight into the techniques needed (Dove et al. 2002). This, undoubtedly, is an increasingly sophisticated and competitive area of activity, no longer one for the well-meaning amateur.

Although development offices are sprouting up on U.K. campuses, it's going to take something of a cultural revolution to get anywhere near the American model. More important than the fundraising techniques themselves is the deep-rooted tradition of giving that exists in this country; quite simply, there is an expectation that one gives back. Indeed, to be seen as uncommitted philanthropically can easily become the basis of public criticism for a contemporary Croesus. And not just with respect to higher education. Donations and benefactions flow into the world of the arts and culture, and that includes libraries (think of that transplanted Scot, Carnegie, and the enduring effects his legacy has had on life and literacy in this country). Families like Rockefeller, Ford, Mellon, Lilly, and Annenberg have become synonymous with strategic giving. In the years to come, however, these august names may be dwarfed by those of Bill and Melinda Gates, whose eponymous $24 billion foundation (www.gatesfoundation.org/) makes hugely significant contributions in a number of areas, nationally and internationally, including, again, the world of public libraries.

Being a transplanted cynic, it's all too easy to mock some of the saccharine language and invasive approaches used by institutional fundraisers in this country, but there is simply no gainsaying the widespread social benefits. The lives of students and citizens are unarguably improved as a result of the staggering generosity of individuals and institutions. And, lest I'm accused of hypocrisy, let me clarify that I am one of the happy beneficiaries of this culture; my Rudy professorship, which I hold as long as I remain at Indiana University, augments both my salary and my personal research funds. So, grateful thanks to the long-deceased James H. Rudy and all the other donors who help feather our nests!

REFERENCES

Dove, K. E., V. L. Martin, K. K. Wilson, M. M. Bonk, and S. C. Beggs. 2002. *Conducting a Successful Development Services Program*. San Francisco: Jossey-Bass.

Pulley, J. L. 2003. "Another Downer of a Year for College Endowments." *Chronicle of Higher Education* (January 24): A23–27.

WHAT A LIBRARY IS NOT

Originally published November 2002

What is a library? According to my dictionary it is "a place in which literary, musical, artistic, or reference materials . . . are kept for use but not for sale." This is a noncontentious, bare-bones description of a familiar institution, one that, I imagine, would pass muster with professional and lay readers alike. But, as I hear accounts of patrons viewing pornography on library terminals and read stories in *Library Journal* (*LJ*) and elsewhere with headlines such as "Barefoot Patron Sues Library," I sometimes wonder whether sanity has gone out the library's back door, and whether we have lost sight of the commonly understood purpose of this venerable institution.

Let me, therefore, enumerate a number of things that a library is not, and if in so doing I offend your sensibilities, so be it, for this is, increasingly, the quotidian reality in parts of the nation. A library is not a community masturbation center; a library is not a porn parlor; a library is not a refuge for the homeless; a library is not a place in which to defecate, fornicate, or micturate; a library is not a bathing facility; a library is not a dumping ground for latchkey children. There you have it, straight from the hip. You may find these statements distasteful, not to mention blindingly obvious, but anecdotal and other evidence suggests that such quirky and deviant practices are depressingly common in our urban libraries. Indeed, the perpetrators of said behaviors have been blessed with the wonderful euphemism, "atypical patrons." This,

35

in turn, has given rise to workshops on "atypical patron behavior." "Never mind the root cause, let's concentrate on the symptoms" is the unspoken motto. Meanwhile, the Equal Employment Opportunity Commission (EEOC) has just suggested that the Minneapolis Public Library pay twelve employees $75,000 each in damages for having suffered from exposure to heavy porn surfing by patrons, and library staffers at the Ottawa Public Library have filed grievances through the Canadian Union of Public Employees regarding their institution's unfettered Internet access policy. Where will permissive policies and temporizing bring us?

As it happens, I am writing this column after talking to an experienced reference librarian from one of the nation's larger urban library systems. He tellingly used the phrase "barnyard behaviors" to describe the miscellany of antisocial practices sketched above, practices which occur with regularity not only in his but also other libraries. Let me make one thing clear: my friend is not devoid of a social conscience or bereft of basic human compassion, nor is it that he doesn't understand the larger economic forces and government policies that have created this kind of social fall-out. It's just that he doesn't feel that it is the library's responsibility to act as a default social welfare agency. Libraries, as the definition I quoted above makes clear, are not shelters, and librarians, by extension, should not be viewed as surrogate social workers—nor should they risk practicing social work without a license.

According to another story I read on *LJ*'s website, Tacoma's Public Library's central facility has become a refuge for the local homeless population (as many as one thousand homeless are spending daylight hours in the library), with the result that the administration has instituted a policy restricting patrons from bringing "bedrolls, big boxes, or bulky bags into the library." See library-journal.reviewsnews.com. Why in heaven's name has it reached this point? I don't take a bedroll when I go to the opera (though, come to think of it, if it's Wagner's *Ring Cycle* I probably should), I don't take big boxes when I visit Borders, and I don't take bulky bags into the Tate Modern. This strikes me as an eminently sensible ordinance, designed to ensure that the library functions as, well, a library. This is not management by stigmatization; it's good old-fashioned common sense. But good, old-fashioned common sense isn't sufficient anymore because to speak the unpleasant truth is to risk condemnation by those who should know better.

Social inclusion is a noble goal and sound public policy, but it should not be construed as a license to abandon time-honored standards and expectations concerning behavior in public spaces such as libraries. The following words, though emblematic of this nation's spirit, were not meant to be interpreted literally by library administrators:

> Give me your tired, your poor.
> Your huddled masses yearning to breathe free,
> The wretched refuse of your teeming shores.
> Send these, the homeless, tempest-tost to me
> I lift my lamp beside the golden door.

This extraordinary invitation is, of course, found on the Statue of Liberty, and it is there—not above the porticos of America's public libraries—that it should remain.

It seems to me and a few others that a disruptive minority is effectively preventing the majority of bona fide library patrons from exercising their rights. Once again, it is a case of the politically correct tail wagging the socially responsible dog. It's high time this issue was raised and discussed systematically within the profession and with locally elected politicians. It's simply too important to be brushed under the stained carpet.

BAREFACEDLY BAREFOOTED

My "What a Library Is Not" column generated the largest response of any opinion piece I've published over the years. It was as if it had tapped a hidden nerve. In this essay, I'll let the voices of some of my correspondents speak for themselves—anonymously, since several said that they did not feel they could make their views known publicly (that in itself is a most revealing insight into the realities of professional life in the nation's libraries).

From Texas: "I'm so glad that finally someone of your stature is saying what those of us in the trenches have been saying for a long time. . . . I know of quite a few colleagues who have left the profession because of this and there must be some discussion of this issue—it is too important." From New Jersey: "Thanks so much for your recent article in *Library Journal* saying aloud what we've all been muttering under our breaths for years!" From Ohio: "You are absolutely 'right on' in decrying the absence of common sense among library administrators in forthrightly and consistently demanding that commonly accepted standards of public behavior be required in library buildings." From Colorado: "If anything, your article shows restraint in describing the often zoo-like atmosphere of public libraries. Your article is making the rounds at the library I work at. Most of us are nodding our heads in agreement." From Indiana: "It's rare to never that your commonsense approach to library management—that of requiring acceptable behavior—is seen in *LJ*. I no longer work in public service because of the experiences you described in your piece. . . . ALA, as with the pornography issue, refuses to listen to librarians on the front lines dealing with these problems day to day." From California: "I was so heartened by your column. You voiced all the sentiments that I have had for years and years. . . . please write more about liberating your library for your community and your staff." From Canada: "I cannot thank you enough for speaking for the majority of us, when you wrote your piece in the November 15 edition of *Library Journal*. Well said and well done." From Texas (where they don't mince words): "I have been waiting 30 + years for someone with the balls to write this commentary. Thank you." From Ohio: "I just wanted to tell you that I thought your most recent article about problem patrons and their behavior was excellent. I . . . was pleasantly shocked by the frank language. Keep shooting from the hip." From Indiana: "I liked your column very much, it touches on a number of serious issues we as a profession seem not to want to discuss, I am afraid that by trying desperately to be all things to all people, libraries risk ending up being nothing to everyone." From New York (and this one was published in *Library Journal*): "The 'disruptive minority' is intimidating the majority, who are running to Barnes & Noble and the like. There, the carpets are clean, the air does not reek, and customers are not staring, eyes glazed, at explicit Internet sites/sights. Librarians no longer 'shush' patrons; instead, we tiptoe around their 'barnyard behavior.' Dare we take a stand? Thank you Blaise Cronin for suggesting that it is long overdue." From Missouri (also published in *LJ*): "Sadly Blaise Cronin's blindingly blunt portrait exactly describes the environment I am victimized by every working day. Thank you, Cronin, for saying what had to be said." From Illinois: "I am writing to commend you for the article in LJ from 11/15 on 'What a Library Is Not.' . . . I hope you will offer more of your thoughts on this topic in the future." From Orgeon: "Great article! I agree with it. However, in my agreement and practicing what I preach about keeping order and fairness in the library, I ran afoul of my now former new, young, ambitious, we-must-welcome-everyone-no-matter-what supervisor, and am now out of a job." And, finally, from Ontario: "I just want to thank you for coming down so clearly on one side of the fence regarding this issue. . . . How to deal with all of this is under constant discussion by our management team and staff, and your article has been forwarded and shared with all of them."

I could go on, but I think the central point is clear. Here is an issue that greatly affects the daily working lives of countless librarians, yet it's treated as if it didn't exist. According to *Library Journal*, Hubert Locke, the former dean of the Daniel J. Evans Graduate School of Public Affairs at the University of Washington, commented publicly that Seattle's temporary central library had become a "domestic space for some of the city's transient, mentally ill and homeless populace" (Locke 2003). He went on to say that "the city has a problem and it shouldn't be one for the library to resolve." How come we don't hear active (or retired) deans of library and information science (LIS) schools or professional leaders talking a little common sense in this regard? In case you haven't noticed, the apparatus of the ALA is engaged with matters of rarefied policy, legalistic abstractions, and Beltway lobbying, while the quotidian concerns of the membership are deemed largely unworthy of attention. That's why we have the bizarre situation of staffers at the Minneapolis Public Library filing a "hostile environment" sexual harassment suit for damages and demanding changes in workplace policies and practices, while the professional association remains silent on the matter of porn in libraries. (For an eye-popping account of what actually goes on in some public spaces, read Wendy Adamson's (2002) "Sex in the City—What Happened at the Minneapolis Public Library.") At the same time, depressingly few LIS faculty and administrators seem capable of saying anything on the record that might be construed as politically incorrect when it comes to the subject of antisocial behavior in America's public libraries. My great regret is that the many personal e-mails I receive are not also finding their way to East Huron Street and/or to the editor of *Library Journal* so that the depth of feeling and concern can be better understood by those who really need to know.

Not everyone, however, was unqualifiedly supportive of the views expressed in "What a Library Is Not." There were dissenting voices, and these caught me on the hop. My innocuous remark about barefoot patrons touched a metacarpal nerve, partly because I seemed to be equating barefootedness with the kinds of deviant practices that have now become indelibly associated with many of this country's urban public libraries. One member of the Society for Barefoot Living (www.barefooters.org) gently explained the rationale for going barefoot and made an intelligent case for greater social tolerance of those who eschew footwear: "In the six years I've spent barefoot I've met quite a lot of others, in person and online, and we're not antisocial people. We're just people like any others who don't like to wear shoes, that's all." Bare feet are hardly a reason to fall out, but whether we like it or not, certain norms and conventions dictate where and when (not to mention why) footwear is deemed desirable or de rigueur, though these are not fixed in stone. I just read somewhere that Hooters, the restaurant chain best known for its comely waitresses, is planning to launch an airline (Hooters Air, www.hooters air.com/about/), while Naked Air (www.naked-air.com/) has announced its first "clothing optional" flight from Miami to Cancun. And according to *Forbes* (Sternstein 2003) a charter airline called Ecstasky Air allows passengers to choose their flight attendants from a pool of 150. There is, of course, a slippery slope argument lurking here. If we let bare feet into the library, where do we draw the clothes line? Topless, bottomless, starkers? Thank goodness I didn't raise the specter of clothing-challenged patrons, or I'd have had the nation's naturists on my back.

REFERENCES

Adamson, W. 2002. "Sex in the City—What Happened at the Minneapolis Public Library." *New Breed Librarian.* www.newbreedlibrarian.org/archives/02.02.apr2002/feature.html [accessed July 23, 2003].

Locke, Hubert. 2003. Quoted here from "Homeless & Transients at Seattle PL Need a New Haven." *Library Journal* (April 10).

Sternstein, Aliya. 2003. "Thongs at 10,000 Meters: Unfasten Your Seatbelts." *Forbes Global Magazine.* http://www.forbes.com/global/2003/0217/047.html [accessed 23 July 2003].

ALL TOO COMMON SCENTS

I thought it must be April Fool's Day. But it wasn't. It was just America being its usual silly self. In the background, ABC's Charles Gibson was being as insufferably perky as I was being routinely sullen. Still, I froze in my slippered tracks. The Massachusetts town of Shutesbury had gone "fragrance-free," according to the grinning Gibson. (Apparently it is not alone in this; a few other communities have embarked on equally self-enlightened courses, while Halifax, Novia Scotia, has, in fact, gone so far as to declare itself a fragrance-free city, trumping humble Shutesbury.) I simply couldn't believe my luck. What at first sounded like a joke turned out to be . . . well, a humongously serious joke.

How, I wondered, could the town administrator, David Ames, have kept a straight face when announcing that Shutesury's public meetings would henceforth be "fragrance-free"? Talk about deadpan. This guy, I reckoned, must surely in a comedic league of his own, or a devotee of wild, East Coast mushrooms. My morning glee was quickly upgraded to ecstasy when I heard that Shutesbury's M. N. Spear Memorial Library would soon be displaying a sign indicating that it had been designated a "fragrance-free zone," as if a public library could be anything other than a fragrance-rich zone, given the nature of its well-thumbed stock and the lifestyles of more than few of its habitués (see "What a Library Is Not" in this volume).

So off to the Web we went, where further investigation revealed that the library would be holding fragrance-free hours on Mondays from 10:30 to noon. The good burghers of Shutesbury were going to be asked to self-segregate on the basis of whether they used perfumes, scented deodorants, or detergents that might just bother their fellow citizens. Apparently, the May 3rd town meeting was going to offer three designated seating areas: one for those who use scented products, one for those who didn't actually use a cologne or some such fragrance that particular day (but occasionally did), and one, I guess, for the naturally scented. Elsewhere I read that there will be an area designated as "seating for those who forgot and used cologne and perfume." The good news, according to Mr. Ames, is that "[w]e're not going to have people standing at the door and sniffing." Just as well, for how could we be sure that the guards themselves would be both 100-percent scent-free and gifted with the necessary ability to detect the unacceptably scented among their fellow men (and women)? "*Quis custodiet ipsos custodes*?" "Who, indeed," I hear you intone, and quite rightly so! Mr. Ames doesn't add whether dogs might be used to sniff out offenders (as the U.S. customs service does with arriving passengers at some ports of entry), but nothing would surprise me anymore. Apparently, according to one Ziporah Hildebrandt, chairwoman of the town's Americans with Disabilities Act (ADA) committee, most people don't seem to realize that their personal care products are scented and that these products can have an effect on the "chemically sensitive." Perhaps the residents of Shutesbury are illiterate or somehow olfactorally challenged, or perhaps they simply live on another planet.

But where, on earth, does one draw the line? I've attended more than my fair share of professional meetings where the acrid mix of natural body odor and halitosis has made me feel like retching. Even the Great and the Good are not above reproach in my experience. If only my colleagues and others had doused themselves with deodorants and (even cheap) perfumes/colognes, I'd have been a much happier man. But in Shutesbury, the artificial is apparently more heinous than the naturally odious. Where, I wonder, will the citizens of Shutesbury and other equally priggish communities draw the proverbial line? What about the aesthetic affront to my sensibilities of a loud necktie, a brassy perm, stubble, farting, belching, or too much rouge on a face past its prime? And what about the stench of political correctness that, figuratively speaking, fills the meeting rooms of academia and turns my stomach?

The citizens of Shutesbury should be introduced to a few home truths. First: "Ordinances cannot compensate for the lack of savoir faire, sound upbringing, and common sense." And second: "The obsession with fragrances may lead to an obsession with other allegedly odious traits and behaviors, the first step on the road to totalitarianism". If we can ostracize those who stink (according to our preferred and rather selective definitions), why not also ostracize those whose views or lifestyles we find morally or ideologically repugnant? In for a penny, in for a fascistic pound. *Quo vadis* Shutesbury?

Burned Any Good Books Lately?

Originally published February 2003

"Pastor's Potter Book Fire Inflames N. Mex. Town." Now there's a sub-editor having a bit of fun. I read the headline three times, each time thinking it said "Potty Pastor's Book Fire." It should have. The accompanying photo in the February 2002 *American Libraries* article shows a clean-cut, prosperous-looking American couple chucking books, among them *Harry Potter*, onto a bonfire.

Pastor Jack Brock and his wife are smiling contentedly as they go about their Monty Pythonish task, aided and abetted (off-camera) by congregants whose enthusiasm for this form of spiritual cleansing went well beyond Ms. Rowling's bestseller to include, most ludicrously, *The Complete Works of William Shakespeare*. In for a penny, in for a pound, as the saying goes. One didn't know whether to laugh or cry, but then I remembered Kansas and creationism, Jerry Falwell and gays. . . .

The Harry Potter books "teach children how they can get into witchcraft," according to the flaming pastor, whose acolytes sang "Amazing Grace" as they went about their pyrotechnic duties. What's worse is that Brock wasn't even the first to go down the media-covered, bonfire route. In March of the previous year, the Rev. George Bender held a burning of "ungodly" books (including, you've guessed it, *Harry Potter*), CDs, and videos somewhere in rural Pennsylvania. Shirley MacLaine (author) and *Pinocchio* (Disney movie) were among those on Bender's bizarre hit list. Church members sang "Amazing Grace" and "Father of Creation," as

Bruce Springsteen and Pearl Jam were consigned ceremoniously to the flames. The story was picked up by Reuters and generated considerable publicity for the burner-in-chief.

Book-burning was in fashion seven decades ago, only then it was called *Bücherverbrennung* and took place in cities throughout Germany. The black-and-white images of *Sturmabteilung* (SA) members giving Nazi salutes as piles of "un-German" books burned on the *Opernplatz* in Berlin on the night of May 10, 1933, are a particularly chilling reminder of where the ill-conceived, attention-seeking actions of a Bender or a Brock can lead. These two men of the cloth would be well advised to heed the oft-quoted words of Heinrich Heine: "Wherever they burn books, they will also, in the end, burn people."

Of course, the Nazis were not alone in burning books or human beings. Heretics, witches, and sundry other unfortunates have long followed, or preceded, books to the flames. In the armamentarium of the fundamentalist fire has been a favorite means of eliciting the truth, cleansing souls, and eradicating the undesirable. Its appeal goes well beyond the symbolic. Sometimes it's easier not to build a bonfire, and simply torch the national or state library, a very effective way of erasing collective memory and weakening national or ethnic identity. On other occasions, the urge to burn may be more modest, merely a desire to eradicate a specific, offending text: centuries ago, Popes Gregory and Julius both issued papal bulls for the burning of the Talmud—precision pyrotechnics, if you will. This, I suppose, is a bit like placing rewards on the heads of al-Qaeda operatives rather than carpet-bombing every nation that is suspected of housing terrorists.

The irony is that firebrands across history have probably done much more in the long run for anticensorship than their own cause. The effect of the Nazi book-burnings on civilized opinion worldwide was immense, not least in the United States. Paul Boyer (2002), for instance, has claimed that book-burnings hardened anti-censorship sentiment in this country. One can only hope that the pathetic parochialism of Brock and Bender will, at the very least, galvanize the thinking public's commitment to anticensorship, whether the target is Teletubbies, Tiny Tim, or the Talmud. Indeed, if I were desperate (perish the thought!), in order to boost the sales of my latest monograph, *Pulp Friction* (2003), I'd suggest that the publisher contract with Pastor Brock and his merry band to organize a rip-roaring burning of my diabolic potboiler, preferably with a CNN or, failing that, C-SPAN camera crew positioned nearby. I'm pretty sure the publicity would work wonders for my royalty payments.

Finally, a request to all misguided librarians up and down the country who feel a need to remove books from their collection: please consider the merits of the "holy bonfire" approach as an alternative to the commonly used stealth method. Be brave. Stand up publicly for your convictions. Come out of the censor's closet. Burn some books . . . with your buddies Brock and Bender.

P.S. The Vatican has recently given J. K. Rowling's Harry Potter series the moral thumbs-up. According to the American Library Association, the series has topped the list of most challenged books for four consecutive years.

REFERENCES

American Libraries. 2002. "Pastor's Potter Book Fire Inflames N. Mex. Town." (February): 18.

Boyer, P. 2002. *Book Censorship in America from the Gilded Age to the Computer Age*. Madison, Wis.: University of Wisconsin Press.

Cronin. B. 2002. *Pulp Friction*. Lanham, Md.: Scarecrow Press.

WOLVES IN SHEEP'S CLOTHING

As a teenager I would spend several weeks of the summer with schoolchildren my own age in the *Gaeltacht* learning to speak the Irish language. It was meant to be an immersion experience. We would go to language classes, stores, dances, and strive to do everything through the medium of Gaelic. That was the intention, but every so often we would lapse into the mother tongue. On one occasion the priest caught us while speaking English, and only an Oscar Award–winning performance of contrition prevented us from being sent straight back to our families for this most venial of sins.

But it was ever thus. In medieval universities, there were language police, the *lupi* (from the Latin for "wolf") whose job was to ensure that the students spoke Latin at all times, the required lingua franca of early academia (Matthews 1997, 116). Today the *lupi* ("loopy" would be more to the point) are at every schoolhouse door around the country, getting their fangs into the textbooks and recreational reading materials that feed our children's minds. And the results, by God (I mean, by gum!) are unspeakably distressing!

How do I know? I've just been reading Diane Ravitch's (2003, xi) devastating exposé of what she, with considerable understatement, calls "the regime of censorship that has quietly spread throughout educational publishing." Apparently, educational publishing is a bit like government procurement. A small number of big publishers vie for multimillion-dollar book contracts with the school boards of the nation's states, of which California and Texas are the most influential in shaping national trends. Success de-

pends in no small measure on satisfying the mind-bogglingly ab-
surd bias and sensitivity criteria fostered by educators and their
censorious allies. (For example, we can no longer say that someone
is "wheelchair bound"; we should instead speak of "a person who
uses a wheelchair.") Ravitch has painstakingly unearthed the
guidelines used by many of the leading publishers, state education
boards, and professional associations and produced a quite breath-
taking glossary of banned words, usages, stereotypes, and topics. If
Orwell had come up with this, we would have accused him of
going over the top for literary effect. The reality is that this country
has already, more or less silently, gone over the top, and big time.
Jay Leno could fuel a week's worth of shows from this book alone.

Across the nation, armies of po-faced (banned, I suppose) bias
and sensitivity reviewers ("And what do you do for a living,
Daddy?") are hacking the soul (banned, I imagine) out of literature and life. Stereotypes (housewives) are to be avoided at all
costs; what would these pipsqueaks make of Philip Larkin's quirky
observations that holidays are "an entirely feminine concept," or
that the poet, Ted Hughes, was like "an Xmas present from Easter
Island?" But there is more: "emotionally charged" topics (witchcraft, for instance) are anathema (which is why poor Harry Potter
continues to have such a hard time with the religious right); negative material (squabbling parents) should be expunged; dinosaurs,
naturally, cannot be mentioned by name (too close to the creation-
ism/evolution controversy); representational fairness is required
(the ethnic mix of characters in a book should reflect national de-
mographics); sexism is verboten(so no more "mankind" and *hasta
la vista* to the Founding Fathers, all of whom just happened to be
. . . men); handicaps don't exist anymore (just ask any quadri-
plegic); and to consider impaired sight, for example, a disability
would be nothing less than an unpardonable instance of bias. Re-
gionalism is also a crime in the eyes of the language police, such
that (and this is one of but many rib-tickling, tear-triggering in-
stances gathered up by Ravitch in her research) a true story about

a young blind man who hiked to the summit of Mount McKinley makes an unacceptable book because it was about hiking and mountain climbing, which, of course, favors students who live in regions where those activities are common and, by the same token, disadvantages those who don't. What a load of codswallop (almost certainly banned)!

If I didn't know better, I'd have thought that Ms. Ravitch had written an elaborate parody. But remember that our university campuses have been strangulated by restrictive speech codes for years, such that the Foundation for Individual Rights in Education (FIRE) is planning to sue public colleges in twelve federal appellate circuits. FIRE maintains that speech codes have not been removed from campuses despite widely held beliefs about their unconstitutionality, but have been incorporated into "sexual-harassment policies, diversity statements, e-mail policies, and student codes of ethics" (McMurtie 2003, A31). FIRE is currently building a website that will list and rate polices at 300 colleges across the country (www.speechcodes.org). This will surely make sorry reading.

In her book, Ravitch lays bare the monstrous perversion of truth and the systematic and pervasive sanitization of reality brought about by the antics of both the extreme left and the far right, coupled with the profit-seeking pusillanimity of the piggies in the middle (the educational publishing conglomerates). Having reviewed a variety of bias and sensitivity guidelines, she concludes depressingly, if obviously, that these latter-day *lupi* "employed a set of assumptions that were outside the realm of what seemed to be common sense" (Ravitch 19). Not for the first time in the pages of *Jeremiad Jottings* (or *Pulp Friction*, for that matter) one can but lament the abandonment of common sense by the ideologues and administrators empowered to make decisions that will have an enduring impact on the lives of successive generations.

These wolves in sheep's clothing need to be driven out mercilessly, and one way to help the cause is to send examples of content

and language censorship to Diane Ravitch at her website (www
.languagepolice.com). Ms. Ravitch has done a sterling job unmask-
ing the insidious influence of the politically correct pedants and
apparatchiks who determine what our children read. The situation
she describes is nothing short of a national tragedy, a clumsy and
deeply pernicious attempt to control our thoughts by controlling
our exposure to offending words and images.

REFERENCES

McMurtie, B. 2003. "War of Words." *Chronicle of Higher Education*
(May 23): A31–32.

Matthews, A. 1997. *Bright College Years: Inside the American Campus
Today.* New York: Simon & Schuster.

Ravitch, D. 2003. *The Language Police: How Pressure Groups Restrict
What Students Learn.* New York: Knopf.

COACH CLASS IN ACADEMIA

Originally published May 2003

First things first. Indiana University (IU) has been reasonably good to me, and the criticism of collegiate athletics that follows is leveled more against the sporting ecosystem of which IU is part, rather than the institution itself. But let me back up a little. In my student days, sporting distinctions were rewarded with what was called a university "blue." The award of a blue was essentially symbolic, rather like the velvet, tasseled caps my grandfather received each time he played rugby for Ireland.

In my day, there were no sponsorship deals, no sport scholarships, no endorsements, no under-the-table payments. I'm not saying there wasn't the odd bit of jiggery-pokery, but, in the main, the amateur ethos (think "Chariots of Fire") prevailed. Today, collegiate athletics is a big (and sometimes downright nasty) business and a source of continuing embarrassment to many members of the professorate. But I'll say no more on that aspect, since the system and its many flaws have been described in great detail by others, among them my IU colleague Murray Sperber (2000) and, more recently in an opinion piece, George Hanford (2003), president emeritus of the College Board.

Mike Davis, IU's head basketball coach, recently signed a multi-year contract. It consists of $800,000 in guaranteed annual income—a sum, I might observe, that would go a long way toward paying the annual School of Library and Information Science (SLIS) faculty salary bill. What does that say about relative institutional/social values? An interesting aspect of Davis's contract is that there is the possibility of an additional incentive payment of almost $140,000 based on game results and the student athletes' grades. If the team's mean grade point average (GPA) exceeds 2.3 (on a four-point scale), more dollars flow to Mr. Davis. (It should be pointed out that the average IU GPA is 3.01.) If the team's GPA is above 3.3, a further bonus kicks in. Last, but not least, Davis will receive $300,000 just for honoring his contract until July 1, 2005. To make matters worse, IU is currently repaying its fired coach, Bobby Knight, $425,000 a year for eight more years as part of a deferred compensation package.

All of this got me thinking. What if I, as dean, had my remuneration tied to the mean GPA of my students, the number of graduating students, the frequency with which doctoral students presented conference papers, the number of National Science Foundation (NSF) grants my faculty secured, my fundraising success, etc.? What if I promised to remain as dean until 2005 in the face of all other blandishments? You get my drift. Obviously, Mary Sue Coleman understands the realities of contractual life; the new president of the University of Michigan has a compensation package that includes a retention bonus of $500,000 if she remains president for the full five years.

Translate such thinking to Libraryland and imagine a scenario in which this kind of performance-related remuneration model is applied aggressively to library directors. Perhaps a high-flying library manager could negotiate along the following lines: (1) a progressive salary increment if circulation figures grow at a compounded annual rate of X percent; (2) a flat-rate bonus if operating costs are pared back by an agreed amount over a two-year period; (3) a one-time merit payment if patron satisfaction levels are shown to have risen beyond a certain threshold by the expiration of the contract; and (4) a bonus if more than Y million dollars is secured for capital and other projects from federal agencies and/ or foundations.

Maybe the time has come to create Libraryland's market equivalent for "academostars," (Spurgin 2001), those high-visibility professors whose talents are in such demand that they can virtually write their own conditions of employment and remuneration. Only the other day I was reading a 2001 report from the U.K. Audit Commission, which noted that since 1992–1993 visits to public libraries in Britain had fallen by 17 percent and loans by almost one quarter. The report also noted that spending on books was down by one third. Could the decline documented by the Audit Commission be arrested and reversed? Perhaps it is now time, in the United Kingdom at least, to move away from nationally negotiated pay scales and introduce radical performance-based measurements for public sector library managers. More generally, it is certainly worth considering whether, how, and at what cost a properly "incentivized" manager (or administrative team) could produce a reversal. Has the time come to create, or recruit, a cadre of turnaround artists—entrepreneurially inclined librarians who combine professional knowledge and business talent—to reinvigorate public sector libraries?

REFERENCES

Audit Commission. 2001. *Building Better Library Services*. www.audit commission.gov.uk/reports/ [accessed May 29, 2003].

Hanford. G. 2003. "We Should Speak the 'Awful Truth' about College Sports. . . ." *Chronicle of Higher Education* (May 30): B10–11.

Sperber, M. 2000. *Beer and Circus: How Big-Time College Sports Is Crippling Undergraduate Education*. New York: Henry Holt.

Spurgin, T. 2001. "The *Times* Magazine and the Academic Megastars." *The Minnesota Review* 52–54:225–38.

THE TROUBLE WITH
TROPHY SPEAKERS

Originally published June 2003

You've seen the indignant headline: "Top library job goes to non-librarian." It can be hard to swallow and does little to boost the profession's self-esteem. Yet, when it comes to inviting keynote speakers, a different logic seems to apply, at least as far as the American Library Association (ALA) is concerned.

In recent years, a number of high-profile individuals have been invited to be Opening General Session Speakers at the ALA's annual meeting. Now I'm not suggesting that the ALA is the only professional organization to tap "big name" speakers to fill such slots—many groups like to bathe in reflected glory—but there is something strangely inconsistent about this practice, given how the profession typically reacts to outsiders appointed to high-visibility positions. By nabbing trophy speakers, the ALA is, for all intents and purposes, admitting that there is no one in, or on the fringes of, the field worthy of the role or capable of providing a suitably lustrous launch to the annual jamboree. If this is the case, it's a depressing admission about the profession's standing, and if it is not the case, then it's a slap in the face to those within the ranks who ought to be stepping up to the podium. Take a moment and ask yourself, is there no one with sufficient charisma, reputation, eloquence, or stature within Libraryland capable of igniting an ALA annual meeting? Absolutely no one?

But that's not the whole story. As if to rub salt into the open

61

wound, your largest professional association pays its distinguished speakers enormous sums for their brief appearances, a point that has not gone unnoticed. Never mind the political brouhaha which surrounded the invitation to General Colin Powell—"War Criminal to Address ALA" was one of the superior headlines in the professional press—some members vocally condemned the ALA for paying Colin Powell a $70,000 speaking fee for his brief turn at the New Orleans meeting. Pause here for a moment. What Mr. Powell received for his roughly one-hour contribution was twice the annual salary of many public sector librarians. (Confession time: I sometimes receive an honorarium for giving keynote and other talks, but you'd need to remove three zeros from the figure above to get close to my going rate.) His hour in the limelight was equated with two years professional effort at the coalface. Celebrity counts for more than pertinence, it seems. As long as we've got a celebrity—someone who, in the words of Daniel Boorstein, is "known for his well-knownness"—all will be fine.

Apparently, the ire over the size of Powell's speaking fee was short-lived, as many ALA councilors publicly opposed the suggestion that such fees be capped at $20,000. The capping proposal was quickly shot down in council; opponents, such as Sally Gardner Reed, noting that, "we need to be spending our time discussing issues of substance, not micromanaging the line items in our budget." In case you don't know, the ALA has an annual budget of approximately $40 million, so this is chump change. The fact that the chump change, or some of it at any rate, comes from your dues really shouldn't matter. The obscenity of the contrast in public valuations is airily brushed aside; it is inappropriate for membership to micromanage the association's affairs.

This is a highly symbolic issue, one that transcends mere micromanagement. What kind of message does it send to professionals and paraprofessionals across the nation about how their own association values what they do? Moreover, this kind of conspicuous consumption sits uncomfortably with the current ALA president's campaign to boost professional remuneration levels. Perhaps it's time to introduce a few sumptuary laws in East Huron Street and have Headquarters lead by example.

My interest in this topic was piqued further by a conversation I had with an ex-ALA president on the subject of trophy speakers. I was inquiring what the ALA had paid Robert Hughes, writer, art critic, and TV presenter, for his opening talk at the 2002 annual meeting in Georgia. If my memory serves me correctly, the number was $80,000, some of which, I believe, may have come out of something called the "President's fund." Mr. Hughes is a fine fellow, erudite and fluent, but what can he possibly say in one hour to a group of librarians that is worth $80,000? He may make you feel good, but so would a massage. In fact, it would probably have been a lot cheaper to pay for everyone in the auditorium to have a professional massage than trolly in Mr. Hughes for a pep rally.

I am not opposed in principle to outsiders being invited on occasion, but I balk at the size of today's honoraria. Whatever you may think of Powell, Hughes, and the others, it is hard to justify the excessive levels of compensation, given the symbolic slight caused by such invitations. This, surely, is a matter worthy of open debate.

P.S. The subject of Powell's talk was "Volunteerism;" the subject of Hughes's address was "Free Libraries." Did they, as they pocketed their easily gotten gains, notice the irony of it all?

FOLLOW THE MONEY

Originally published April 2003

Whether it's al-Qaeda or Enron, the advice remains the same: follow the money. Of course, that is sometimes easier said than done. Both of these rather different organizations have good reason to want to kick over the traces, and both have shown considerable ingenuity in their efforts to hoodwink auditors and investigators. With the American Library Association (ALA), things are, of course, quite different. This is a reputable professional body, one that is publicly committed to the principles of openness and the free flow of information. So, during a light-hearted dinner-table conversation with a sometime president of the association, I took the opportunity to ask whether, and to what extent, membership dues were being used to underwrite the Children's Internet Protection Act (CIPA) legal fund. (Admission: I was an expert witness for the U.S. Department of Justice (DoJ) in this case, and I was cited in the brief submitted to the Supreme Court.) I labeled my informant's response "fuzzy," and my appetite for more information was immediately whetted. The reason for my interest is simple; many public (and other) librarians are opposed to the inflexible and inconsistent stance taken by the ALA on the issue of digital pornography in libraries (Cronin 2003), yet their professional association uses funds generated directly and indirectly by the membership to support an ideologically repellant position.

In 2002 the ALA's executive director stated that CIPA-related "legal fees [were] expected to top $1.7 million" and that "the sus-

tained commitment of librarians from across the profession"
would be vital to the campaign's success. Individual ALA members
are encouraged to make donations to the CIPA Legal Defense
Fund, while various divisions and affiliated organizations have dedicated funds to the national effort. For example, both the Public
Library Association (PLA) and the Freedom to Read Foundation
(FTRF) have committed $100,000 to the cause, while the Ameri-
can Association of Law Libraries (AALL) recently authorized a
$5,000 donation and the New Hampshire Library Association (to
make a grassroots illustration) made a more modest $2,000 pledge.
I find it especially rich that the ALSC (Association of Library Service to Children) dedicated $25,000 to challenge a law designed to
protect . . . children.

Other contributions came from the parent body. At the 2001
ALA midwinter meeting, the executive board "voted to approve
designation of ALA General Fund Net Assets in the amount of
$250,000 and approve withdrawal from the ALA Future Fund of
$250,000; with a repayment plan, including a repayment schedule,
to the Future Fund approved by Fall 2001 to support the legal
action to overturn the Children's Internet Protection Act." At its
November 2002 meeting (*Library Hotline* 2002), the board noted
that the ALA "had already incurred costs of $1,434,596 since the
inception of the CIPA lawsuit" and "committed $500,000 to the
bill and . . . raised donations of $371,048." I may be quite wrong,
but I am guessing that members' dues constitute part of the association's general fund, in which case members should be clearly informed that they are contributing to an action of which they may
disapprove.

Even if it can be shown that membership dues are not used to
support the anti-CIPA campaign, it is nonetheless the case that the
funds being depleted have been generated, directly or indirectly,
by members who buy ALA publications and attend ALA-organized
conferences, training courses, and so forth. Any other interpretation would amount to sophistry. For a very helpful overview of the

costs associated not only with CIPA but also Communications Decency Act (CDA) and Child Online Protection Act (COPA), I recommend you take a look at Mary Minow's 2003 article in *American Libraries*.

There is another minor, though revealing, dimension to this topic. Both the ALA and the DoJ used a number of expert witnesses in mobilizing their positions. Some, myself included, received payment, and, as is the norm, we were required to reveal our hourly remuneration rate as part of the public record. On the ALA side, I was struck by two things: some witnesses contributed their expertise on a pro bono basis (kudos to all concerned), and, secondly, other ALA experts were being paid considerably more than the DoJ's consultants. It would be instructive if the rank-and-file membership, including those making modest but hard-earned personal contributions to the cause, were able to see the hourly billing rates of some of those representing their position. You might be less than thrilled to learn that the $100 check you sent to the fund was worth only half an hour's worth of professional expertise.

REFERENCES

Cronin, B. 2003. *Pulp Friction*. Lanham, Md.: Scarecrow Press.
Library Hotline. Nov. 25, 2002.
Minow, M. 2003. "Who Pays for Free Speech? The Cost of Defending the First Amendment Is Diverting Scarce Resources from Library Services." *American Libraries* (February): 34–38.

Bun Ladies on Bikes

Some serious image-busting is taking place in Libraryland. The January 2003 issue of *Library Journal* includes a photograph of a leather-clad Jenna Miller astride what I take to be a gleaming, chrome-rich Harley Davidson (well, a motorbike of some description), reading, as one invariably does in such situations, a book. In one fell stroke, the bun-lady stereotype is, if not laid to rest, at least slightly dented. Ms. Miller and eleven colleagues, including the library's director, recently posed for an "Easy Readers" (get it?) calendar as part of a two-million-dollar renovation fundraising campaign. No two ways about it, you've got to admire their imagination and spunk. The odd eyebrow may be raised in genteel circles, but so, I expect, will thousands of dollars for a good cause. On its website, *Library Journal* noted that the staff of Ocean County Library in Toms Rivers, New Jersey, was also hoping that their biker blitz would "quash the old milquetoast image of the profession of blue-haired crones shushing patrons." Dream on!

How many times have we heard the media (such as CNN) comment on media overkill, as if they aren't contributing to the very condition they are decrying. It's pretty much like that with the "image thing." By dredging up the topic yet again, I am, of course, ensuring that unhelpful occupational stereotypes and misperceptions are reinforced. But it's hard to resist the subject when *American Libraries* (also in its January 2003 issue) carries a photograph of two pouting servers at Tempe's new Library Bar and Grill, which, in addition to boasting shelves full of books, has bartenders dressed as librarians. One can look at this in two ways: it's either a demeaning portrayal of the profession (a cheap way of attracting attention and laughs . . . maybe even a few customers), or it's a cause for unqualified celebration. After all, the owner could have plumped for sewage workers, bus drivers, teachers, accountants, or neurologists. But no, the librarian trumped all comers. I recommend we look on the bright side.

These two pieces (the latter featured in the monthly "Thus Said" column of *American Libraries*, which captures publicly expressed views of, and comments on, libraries and librarians) piqued my curiosity, so off I went for a quick Google search on the librarian's image. One is immediately struck by the mass of material available on this (for most people) marginal subject. A good general starting point is the Internet Public Library's (www.ipl.org) "Image of Librarians' section. There are also several websites devoted to the subject, including *Image and the Librarian,* originally created by a couple of graduate students at the University of Maryland. It's a useful enough source of opinion and fact that is at once informative and amusing, though it hasn't been updated in the past couple of years. It has sections on stereotypes, professional status, image, librarians in literature, and so on (home.earth link.net/~cyberresearcher/ImageHomepage.htm). However, if you want to know how librarians are represented in hardcore pornographic paperback novels, you'll need to point your browser to www.riverofdata.com/librariana/porn/, where you'll find a short but interesting exposition that formed the basis of a paper presented at the 1990 Conference of the Popular Culture Association/ American Culture Association in Toronto.

I next visited *NewBreed Librarian* (sounds like something you'd enter at Westminster or Crufts, come to think of it) that had a feature article entitled "The Perception of Image and Status in the Library Profession" (www.newbreedlibrarian.org/archives/01.04.aug 2001/feature1.html). The first page of this piece concludes with some solemnity: "Obsession with image and internalization of negative stereotypical images have caused librarians to doubt the worthiness of the profession as a whole. It's not the stereotype that's the problem, it's the *obsession* with the stereotype." Author Deirdre Dupré goes on to say that we should relegate "the physical-image stereotyping to nothing more than a joke," just, no doubt, as lawyers do when they're called sharks, scumbags, ambulance chasers, and slimeballs.

The more one reads, the harder it is to escape the feeling that the profession is fighting a losing battle; the stereotype is deep-rooted, ubiquitous, and all-too-easily and frequently reinforced. For instance, Carolyn Kirkendall (1986, 40) mentions the characteristics of a librarian as revealed in a 1981 survey carried out for the TV game show *Family Feud*: librarians are: (1) quiet, (2) mean or stern, (3) single and unmarried, (4) stuffy, and (5) wear glasses. Not fun reading if you're one of the tribe, but that's life. One certainly doesn't get the impression that the situation has changed much in the intervening years, judging by my evening's surfing on the Web.

Inevitably, the doom and gloom was bound to spark a reaction. Enter the frolicking Lipstick Librarian (www.lipsticklibrarian.com) and the Gallery of Bellydancing Librarians (www.sonic.net/~erisw/bdlibgallery.html), two sites designed, in different ways, to challenge the persistent stereotype of the bun-wearing (female) librarian. As the URLs will prove, I am not making these up; sometimes truth is, indeed, stranger than fiction, especially in Library-land. Although a great deal has been written on the subject of the occupational stereotype, Margaret Slater's 1979 book remains a very good source of insight, in particular chapters 7 and 8, "The Public Image" and "Reflections: Media as Mirrors." What she has to say won't brighten your day, but remember, if you don't like the negative connotations of librarianship, just think how those lawyers must feel.

Which brings me to Katherine Adams's (2000, 292) article on the "loveless frump" in, of all places, the august *Library Quarterly* (*LQ*). Drawing (with a straight face) on poststructural theories of signification, Ms. Adams recommends that librarians "take on stereotypical characteristics in order to diffuse and disarm the power dynamic that created them in the first place," just as African Americans are "reclaiming the 'N' word, gays and lesbians appropriating the term 'queer,' large women proudly self-identifying as 'fat,' and feminists strategically deploying the term 'bitch.'" In other words: flaunt your inner frump! I'd like to think that the author was speaking tongue-in-cheek, but experience has taught me otherwise. What makes matters worse is that this kind of nonsense has wormed its way into the pages of *LQ*, a journal that purports to publish scholarship.

REFERENCES

Adams, K. C. 2000. "Loveless Frump as Hip and Sexy Party Girl: A Reevaluation of the Old-Maid Stereotype." *Library Quarterly* 70, no. 3:287–301.

Kirkendall, C. A. 1986. "Of Princess Di, Richard Dawson, and *The Book Review Digest.*" *Research Strategies* 4:40–42.

Slater, M. 1979. *Career Patterns and the Occupational Image*. London: Aslib.

RESPONSIBLE, *MOI?*

You're gonna sue McDonald's because their burgers made you fat?
Welcome to America! Some New York teenagers know who is responsible for their being overweight and have responded in time-
honored fashion by slapping lawsuits on the unfortunate fast-food
chain. Fifteen-year-old Gregory Rhymes, who weighs in at 400
lbs., likes to "super-size" his orders at McDonalds, but apparently
sees no connection between his eating habits and his avoir du pois.
You develop emphysema, so you take the cigarette manufacturer
to court in pursuit of a seven-figure settlement. Never mind the
words of the U.S. Surgeon General, which are emblazoned across
the pack, or that anyone who's been awake for the last God-knows-
how-many decades is aware that smoking is not the best way of
ensuring longevity. Public health costs attributable to obesity in
the United States are monstrous, running at about $117 billion an-
nually, compared with $140 billion for smoking (Parlott 2003). Mr.
Rhymes's personal excesses translate all too easily into social costs
to be borne by the rest of us.

This, it appears, is the American way. Offload all responsibility
onto the Other and call in an army of attorneys. And it's not just in
the realm of tobacco. Litigants are showing great imagination of
late. A disgruntled 350-lb. female driver recently tried—
unsuccessfully I'm pleased to report—to make Honda provide her
with a seat belt extender for her Odyssey. And if I were a betting
man, I'd wager that a class-action lawsuit is imminent against
Southwest Airlines, which forces customers who cannot fit into a
regular airline seat to pay for two. By way of an aside, obesity in the

air is a very real safety issue, as I have just discovered. According to the *Sunday Times* (2003, 16), the Federal Aviation Authority (FAA) is considering increasing the average passenger weights used by airlines when calculating load as a result of a fatal crash involving a small regional aircraft in North Carolina earlier this year. The FAA's standard reference weight of 80 kg. per passenger may need to be raised to 88 kg. (which translates to 180 and 190 pounds, respectively).

What is so astonishing is that lawsuits, which most rational folks would deem frivolous, are filed in earnest and with great seriousness of media mien by the offended parties. I, for one, am bewildered. So, too, is Marilyn Vos Savant, who notes with admirable economy of logic and words that "burgers don't make you fat, eating too many of them does." These are not your run-of-the-mill vexatious litigants, but morally outraged victims of capitalist greed and corporate manipulation, who are apparently incapable of taking responsibility for their actions and the choices they make in life. Fortunately, in January 2003 Judge Robert Sweet dismissed the first lawsuit filed against McDonald's with the sage words: "Nobody is forced to eat at McDonald's."

Let's be blunt: America is the grossest nation on earth (Critser 2003), yet it's politically incorrect to call a fat person fat. Actually, it's even worse than that. Believe it or not, I was recently taken to task on the FEMINIST listserv (see "He May Be Retro but [He's] Not Done Spewing" in this volume) for using the word "solid" in an op-ed column to describe three ladies who quite visibly warranted the neutral epithet "solid." Since when did "solid" become a nonword (see also "Wolves in Sheep's Clothing")? It's almost as bad as the preposterous and linguistically misguided attempt to ban the use of the adjective "niggardly" because of its phonetic association with root of the N-word, of which—if we're Caucasian, that is—we can no longer speak. We live in a crazy world where fat people are not fat, where using harmless adjectives constitutes "lookism," where overindulgence is invariably someone else's fault, and where obesity counseling has become a bona fide career option. I sometimes think that the 1973 movie *La Grande Bouffe* is the perfect allegory of contemporary USA—provided we substitute junk food for haute cuisine.

But don't just take my word; take the word of the man to whom the ALA paid $80,000 for a one-hour lecture (see "The Trouble with Trophy Speakers" in this volume). In his delightfully provocative book, *A Culture of Complaint,* Robert Hughes highlights "the old American habit of euphemism, circumlocution, and desperate confusion about etiquette, produced by fear that the concrete will give offense" (1994, 26). Well, obesity is obesity, and if a little linguistic precision can promote intelligent dietary practices, then it's socially justifiable—even if some people choose to take umbrage (members.tripod.com/ss_bbw_ca/fat/pubs.html).

I embarked on this philippic not just because I find the public debate surrounding obesity fascinating in its own right, or because I think governments should penalize the obese (see Liddle's [2003] amusing broadside against the nanny state in this regard), but because it got me thinking about the kind of suits that wackos might file against libraries. This, I readily concede, may constitute the reductio ad absurdum of plaintiff power, but in this litigious nation nothing is beyond the bounds of possibility, so a cautionary review is in order. Consider the following only slightly tongue-in-cheek possibilities:

Scenario #1: A group of patrons files a class action lawsuit against the public library because of the mood-depressing effects experienced by readers as a result of sitting for hours on end under fluorescent lighting.

Scenario #2: The mother of an overweight adolescent sues the local public library because it affords her child unlimited opportunity for sedentary behavior resulting in weight increase and a general lack of physical fitness.

Scenario #3: Information provided by the reference library to a local business is found to be inaccurate, and the library is held liable and prosecuted for professional malpractice.

Scenario #4: A conservative pressure group files a lawsuit against a public library, citing the adverse effects of ambient exposure to digital pornography on both readers and library staff.

Scenario #5: A patron who, every day for years, has used computers in the university library sues the institution because of progressive vision loss resulting from excessive time spent reading from a monitor.

Need I go on? The possibilities are limited only by the imagination and, it goes without saying, lawyerly greed. The best is yet to come, mark my words.

REFERENCES

Critser, G. 2003. *Fat Land: How Americans Became the Fattest People in the World*. New York: Houghton Mifflin.

Hughes, R. 1994. *A Culture of Complaint*. New York: Warner Books.

Liddle, R. 2003. "The Government Is Addicted to Persecuting Fat Slobs Who Smoke." *Spectator* (June 7): 35.

Parloff, R. 2003. "Is Fat the Next Tobacco?" *Fortune* (February 3): 51–54.

Sunday Times. 2003. "Airlines Weigh Up Ways of Dealing With Fat Americans." (May 18): 16.

EGYPT'S WHITE ELEPHANT

Once upon a time there was a great library in Egypt. It was the stuff of legend. The Ptolemaic library in the port city of Alexandria, along with its collection of papyri, was destroyed more than 1,400 years ago, set on fire, many historians believe, by Julius Caesar. And that was the end of the story, or so most of us assumed.

Not so. Phoenixlike, the Bibliotheca Alexandrina has recently risen from the ashes, a resplendent $200 million construction on the Mediterranean's edge. This hefty figure, by the way, does not include the acquisitions budget or staffing expenses. The rebuilding project, led by the Norwegian architectural firm Snoehetta, has taken more than a few years and considerable effort from many organizations and individuals to bring to fruition. Without the sponsorship of UNESCO, the project would never have gotten off the ground. Support, both financial and in-kind, also came from governments around the world; Arab nations contributed about $65 million (Saddam Hussein reportedly coughed up $21 million).

The library's local paladin is Suzanne Mubarek, wife of Egypt's president, and this is her pet cultural project—a situation that can create problems. There are perceptions: first that the library will benefit the elites, and second that funds are being siphoned from much needed social programs to bankroll the Biblioteca (Anderson 2002), to say nothing of the fact that this investment dwarfs routine library-related expenditures in the rest of the country.

I have had no involvement with the Bibliotheca Alexandrina project, and what little I know has been gleaned in the main from journalistic sources, but since day one I have been puzzled as to

77

why anyone in his right mind would want to recreate this particular legend. Simply put, the greatness of yore cannot be recaptured in bricks and mortar. If it could, faded but fabled centers of learning such as Timbuktu would be queuing up for UNESCO construction funds. The ancient library's renown was a function of place and time; the time has passed and place matters less in the digital library age. Alexandria will not likely recapture its historic role as a center of learning simply by laying concrete, chiseling granite blocks, and erecting swathes of coruscating steel and glass.

A library is more than a resplendent superstructure. Yet, a persistent problem with this project has been the lack of books plus the fact that too many have come in the form of donations. Staff recruiting, training, and remuneration are other bones of contention. After ten years of planning and considerable capital investment, the library has in the region of half a million titles, less than a tenth of its planned capacity. What is more, the Bibliotheca Alexandrina is supposed to be "a showpiece for the library in the electronic age" (according to the International Friends of the Alexandria Library, www.ifla.org/IV/ifla68/papers/poster17.htm), though one might respectfully point out that its technological capabilities would likely be put to shame by almost any library in the Association of Research Libraries' (ARL) annual rankings. Is this promotional hype or self-delusion, and who is fooling whom?

Apart from the historic association, it's hard to see why UNESCO felt compelled to invest money and resources on such a scale in Alexandria. Today, this is not one of the world's great centers of learning, commerce, or culture; it's not even a capital city. What logic dictated the concentration of so many scare resources in such an improbable location, moreover one in a politically unstable nation? And what contingencies are in place for the time when UNESCO finally ends its role as midwife? Who will ensure that top-quality staff are hired, the acquisitions budget is maintained, the technological infrastructure is upgraded, and digital records are preserved? And how will a project that is so closely iden-

tified with one individual, First Lady Mubarek, fare when her
patronage is no more? One cannot but wonder about the fragility
of this nascent institution, once the motley international crew of
funders, sponsors, consultants, and well-intentioned friends re-
cedes from the picture and the novelty has worn off.

As I watched over the years from the cornfields of the Midwest,
I was mesmerized by this exercise in atavistic gigantism. The land-
scapes of many Third World nations are littered with architectural
and other follies, testimonies to the vanities of short-lived or short-
serving presidents and irresponsible donors. I shall be pleasantly
surprised if the Bibliotheca Alexandrina lives up to its promoters'
extravagant dreams, but I fear we are looking at a spectacular
white elephant in the making. I hope that those well-remunerated
career bureaucrats who committed UNESCO funds to this ven-
ture will be around to defend publicly their investment decisions,
should my pessimism prove to be warranted.

REFERENCE

Anderson, M. K. 2002. "Raising Alexandria Library." *Wired News*. http://
www.wired.com/news/culture/0,1284,52028,00.html, April 25 [ac-
cessed March 26, 2003].

ASLIB: A VERY SPECIAL ASSOCIATION

Permit me a trip down memory lane. You probably know The Association for Special Libraries and Information Bureau (Aslib) best as a British publisher of monographs, directories, and journals dealing with information science, documentation, knowledge management, and related subjects. Aslib is an acronym first, a proper or trade name second. Indeed, during the economically harsh 1980s, Aslib rebranded itself the Association for Information Management as part of a repositioning strategy. The result, if nothing else, was nominal confusion: an acronym that didn't stand for anything.

Aslib was founded in the 1920s to improve the acquisition, handling, and dissemination of scientific, technical, and industrial information in the United Kingdom (Hutton 1945). In some regards, Aslib was the British equivalent of the Special Libraries Association (SLA) in this country, but there were (and are) important differences. Most significantly, perhaps, Aslib was a nationally and internationally recognized center for information science research, and its in-house team of full-time researchers and consultants (of which I was once one) carried out a range of basic and applied research projects for a wide variety of clients (e.g., trade associations, research councils, nongovernmental organizations, corporations). The other distinguishing feature of Aslib was that it didn't just publish a portfolio of reputable professional journals (e.g., *Aslib Proceedings* and *Program*), but was home to one of the most prestigious scholarly journals in the field of information science, the *Journal of Documentation* (*J. Doc.*), established almost sixty years ago.

For me, Aslib's *intellectual* history is largely synonymous with the activities of the Research and Development (R&D) Department and the scholarly influence of *J.Doc.* Sadly, the R&D Department was shuttered in the late 1980s and *J.Doc.* was sold to a commercial publisher last year. Think of it as a self-inflicted full-frontal lobotomy. Almost all members of the *J.Doc.* editorial board—a board that was atypical in that we met face-to-face four times a years to discuss every paper submitted to the journal—resigned en masse shortly after the sale of the journal was announced, an expression of our collective disapproval of the way in which the sale was conducted and concern for the future integrity of what had been one of the preeminent journals in the history of information science. It's already clear (to me at least) that *J.Doc.* and its replacement board are not what they used to be.

Of course, it is easy to be critical, and, in fairness, Aslib's various directors have had to face tough financial challenges over the years. It cannot have been easy managing a 1920s child in the turbulent business environment of the late twentieth century (Aslib is a registered charity, by the way), so it's not altogether surprising that the family silver had to be sold. Perhaps the erstwhile Association of Special Libraries and Information Bureau has become something of an anachronism in the digital age. Without its "brain" (a.k.a. the Research and Development [R&D] department), Aslib is a small professional association (most of Aslib's 1,500 or so members worldwide are organizations, not individuals) with a relatively modest portfolio of training and publication activities. Whether Aslib can remain independent remains to be seen; recently, after lengthy negotiations, the Institute of Information Scientists merged with the Library Association in a joint effort to remain viable players on the U.K. professional landscape (imagine the American Society for Information Science and Technology merging with the American Library Association). This, surely, is a sign of the times. Meanwhile Aslib continues to go it alone.

I joined Aslib's R&D Department twenty-three years ago. We were seventeen in number and based in a splendid Georgian house in central London, physically separate from the organization's operating headquarters in the even more salubrious Belgrave Square. The atmosphere was intellectually stimulating, as you'd expect with a group of dedicated information science researchers drawn from a diversity of backgrounds. I know of no equivalent organization in our field comprising such a concentration of researchers. By way of illustration, Professors Brian Vickery (University College, London), Stephen Roberston (City University, London), and myself (University of Strathclyde) all served time in Aslib's R&D department before being appointed to their chairs in information science.

Aslib was also a pioneer in organizing information science and information management conferences—a market that now suffers from overcapacity—with the incomparable Elisabeth Lowry-Corry at the helm. Those were the halcyon days, and even if I arrived at the twilight stage I was well aware of my good fortune. But for Aslib, my career would have taken a quite different and, undoubtedly, less interesting turn. It is a shame that the organization has lost its brain and its soul, but such, if I may resort to cliché, is life. In some respects, Aslib's R&D Department was a one-of-a-kind think tank for the information science community, a forerunner of the many university-based research centers in information science and cognate subjects that have emerged in the last twenty to twenty-five years. Should the R&D Department not have been retained? Should *J.Doc.* and the publishing business have been sold? I like to think not, but then I didn't have the unenviable task of balancing the books. If you'd like to hear both sides of what has proved to be, at times, a disputatious story, read Richard Poynder's (2003) account, which includes stinging criticism from, among others, yours truly along with robust rejoinders from Aslib's mettlesome director, Roger Bowes.

REFERENCES

Hutton, R. S. 1945. "The Origin and History of Aslib." *Journal of Documentation* 1, no. 1:6–20.

Poynder, R. 2003. "Surviving in a Harsh World." *Information Today* 20, no. 4:1, 64, 66, 68–70.

THE PUBLIC INTELLECTUAL

Originally published January 2003

We reflexively associate public intellectuals with France, a country that not only produces iconic figures (such as Jean-Paul Sartre or Pierre Bourdieu) but also seems to revere the species. I sense that public intellectuals are less common and much less respected in other nations, although I do recall from my youth the high visibility of philosophes such as Bertrand Russell, Marganita Laski, and Arthur Koester on British television and in the media more generally. Not so long ago I saw the sociologist Anthony Giddens (former director of the London School of Economics) described in the *Times Higher Education Supplement* as "one of our few genuine intellectuals," which caused me to reflect on who else might make a list of British public intellectuals. I'm still reflecting.

To be sure, one can easily name scholars and others who are visible in the media and able to talk about a topic on demand. However, the public intellectual as defined by Richard Posner is not synonymous with the specialist or subject expert but is someone whose views are accessible to the layman and whose focus is on wide-ranging issues of general public concern. This, of course, rules out the likes of Derrida and other postmodern theorists whose obscurity of style "is a source of their charisma" (Posner 2001, 27). According to Posner, public intellectuals are often, but not necessarily, academics; Noam Chomsky is, but Susan Sontag, whom Terry Eagleton, no mean intellectual himself, recently singled out as this county's most complete public intellectual, is not. Typically, they are, in Posner's words, "controversialists, with a tendency to take extreme positions . . . often careless with facts and rash in predictions" (35).

Richard Posner's ambitious dissection of the public intellectual is much more than a lament for the good old days or a discursive account of a presumptively dying breed. Rather, being a chap of formidable intellect and erudition, one who elegantly instantiates his own working definition of public intellectual, Posner begins with a rigorous economic analysis (both demand- and supply-side) of the marketplace for pundits, soothsayers, and bona fide intellectuals. "Writing for an incurably undiscriminating public, the modern public intellectual is likely to find his readers mostly among persons predisposed to agree with him" (81). George Steiner, in other words, is less likely to get the ink or grab more eyeballs than Jane Fonda or Bono expatiating on the cause of the day. These celebrity pundits are certainly easier to absorb than a polyglot scholar of the Steinerian ilk.

Posner wants to know whether the aggregate utterings of these so-called public intellectuals have "truth value," as opposed to entertainment value. Bono's heart is unquestionably in the right place when it comes to Third World debt relief, but can we always trust what the Irish rock singer tells us, and does he add value to public understanding of the complex of issues? Posner doesn't use Bono as a case in point; instead he examines the quality of commentary offered by such notables as Noam Chomsky (linguistics) and the late Stephen Jay Gould (biology) on subjects outside their core areas of professional competence and notes with concern the "casualness with which evidence is handled in much public-intellectual work because of the absence of the usual gatekeepers who filter and police academic publication" (99).

At the heart of Posner's stimulating book there is a statistical analysis of the modern public intellectual, based upon frequency of media mentions. Bibliometricians will not be surprised to find that celebrity is unevenly distributed across the population of public intellectuals. As Posner puts it, "Fans tend to coalesce around a handful of 'stars,' people who are not necessarily the best in their field . . . but whose vivid personalities make them apt focal points for like-minded people to organize around" (176–77). Perhaps the most interesting part of Posner's analysis is the comparison of (1) media mentions (using LexisNexis), (2) Web mentions (using Google), and (3) scholarly citations (using the Institute for Scientific Information (ISI)'s citation databases). Posner wants to know if scholarly impact correlates positively with either media mentions or Web salience, or, to put it another way, do those who win the "citations derby" (184) also finish in the vanguard of the media stakes? The answer is a fairly resounding "no." It's worth noting that all of Posner's data and statistical analyses are freely available on his on his website at the University of Chicago, where he is a visiting scholar when not serving as a judge on the U.S. Court of Appeals for the seventh circuit.

Much of the second half of Posner's *Public Intellectuals* is an in-depth analysis of "selected public-intellectual expressive genres" (223), ranging from philosophy/literary criticism (Martha Nussbaum) through political satire (Aldous Huxley) to law (Richard Dworkin). These chapters bring to life some of the issues, tropes, and tactics deployed by a variety of public intellectuals and, at the same time, show off the author's formidable forensic skills. Overall, Posner is critical of the contemporary public intellectual, and appropriately, if fancifully, the book's concluding section lists some proposals for improving a market in which dubious goods are served up by putative experts with limited knowledge of the subject upon which they have been asked, or have chosen, to pontificate. Posner is not so naïve as to imagine that today's successful public intellectuals will have to justify their predictions or publicly retract erroneous statements, for, as he tellingly notes, "the irresponsibility of public-intellectual work is one of the rewards of being a public intellectual" (396). This is just one of the peculiarities of the contemporary market for public intellectuals penetratingly analyzed by Posner.

Reading this book raised the inevitable question: "Are there any public intellectuals within the ranks of the library and information science field?" The short answer to this is a definite and depressing "no"—at least based on the results of a small study I conducted with my colleague Debora Shaw (Cronin and Shaw 2002). Even the most highly cited individuals in our field (those, for the sake of argument, whose work has the most scholarly impact) are virtually invisible in the mainstream media. In sum, the voices of Library and Information Science (LIS) faculty are inaudible in the public domain. Although some professors' names may appear with frequency on the Web, the sources of and motivations for those invocations are so varied that it's difficult to say just what is being measured.

Our findings suggest that the field is simply not producing its quota of public intellectuals and philosophes—scholars who move effortlessly between the groves of academe and the public sphere. The closest we come is the Librarian of Congress, be it Daniel Boorstein or James Billington, but, strictly speaking, these eminences are outsiders—scholars who just happen to be political appointees at the field's apex. The LIS world has no spokespersons of its own who contribute influentially to national debates on the issues of the day, whose pronouncements help mold public opinion. Where, one has to ask, is our homegrown answer to the Nicholson Bakers of this world?

Given that the profession likes to see itself at the vanguard of democratic values and social inclusion, this silence is all the more perplexing. Perhaps we should think about how we could recruit more visible and high-minded individuals into the profession. Suggestions welcome.

REFERENCES

Cronin, B., and D. Shaw. 2002. "Banking (on) Different Forms of Symbolic Capital." *Journal of the American Society for Information Science & Technology* 53, no. 13:1267–70.

Posner, R. A. 2001. *Public Intellectuals: A Study of Decline*. Cambridge, Mass.: Harvard University Press.

SIGNS OF THE TIMES

Flash back to the State of the Union Address. Zoom in on President Bush's jacket. There it is: a lapel pin, which, as far as I could tell, is an American flag. These days, politicians and executives scarcely dare to appear publicly without at least one thematically appropriate lapel pin. Some wear two, and I pretty sure I've seen a few with three festooned on their overworked lapels. Before we so much as think about the semiotics of lapel pins and such, let me make my position on this issue absolutely clear: lapel pins are right up there with buttons (what I called badges in my childhood) and other inherently puerile and sartorially reprehensible artifacts that can be appended to one's outer garments.

It's one thing to wear the odd military medal or royal decoration, but festooning oneself (especially if one is an adult) with lapel pins is simply not on. National pride is to be admired, but lapel pins trivialize the underlying sentiment. Let Old Glory fly proudly at full staff wherever appropriate, and bring on pomp and circumstance when the occasion demands it, but don't drag pride in one's nation down to the abject level of lapel pins. National pride deserves something more than a fistful of freebies from a governmental schwag bag or the wearing of any one of the staggering array of commercially available pins. Did you know there are dozens of patriotic pins, ranging from a variety of U.S. flags, to law enforcement and military badges, to so-called awareness pins and institution/building-specific ones (e.g., the World Trade Center, Pentagon)? Perhaps this is not altogether surprising. In a recent essay in *The New Yorker*, Simon Schama (2003) captures the country's well-established predilection for flag waving, medals, marching bands, and loudmouthed patriotism. But the market for lapel pins extends way beyond patriotism; you can order customized lapel pins for any subject or event and choose from a range of forms (e.g., die struck, cloisonné, photo etched). It's a totem collector's dream come true.

Sad to say, the outbreak of lapel pins has spread well beyond the realm of patriotism. Grown men and women, in industry and academia, now routinely bristle with pins proclaiming their institutional affiliations. I've seen senior administrators at my own university wear these daft decorations. We all know who they are; they, presumably, know who they are, and their institutional affiliation is common knowledge, so why resort to these pinprick identity reinforcers? Who's impressed? Who notices? Who cares? Real grown-ups don't wear lapel pins; kids do, train spotters do, and, perhaps, even the odd hippie does. Lapel pins are not, and never will be, cool. These tacky talismans suggest insecurity and a naïve belief that such a mindless form of semaphore could have any effect upon the intelligent observer. They signal limply that the wearer subscribes to, cares about, or belongs to this or that . . . and how about you?

The day after President Bush's State of the Union address, one of my colleagues in School of Library and Information Science (SLIS) turned up at a faculty meeting wearing, proudly I can only surmise, a word mark (that, I believe, is the official term for this subgenre of pin) for the Indiana University School of Informatics—not SLIS. Was this good soul making a super subtle semiotic point, or was he struggling with some form of personal identity crisis? Who knows, but the suavely suppressed sniggers of my colleagues said it all.

What are we to make of Hillary Clinton's wearing of a lapel pin featuring the Phoenix Bird, one of the foremost symbols of the Illuminati? The answer is simple, according to a bizarre website I stumbled across: Bill and Hillary Clinton are practicing Illuminist witches—whatever that may mean. Be warned; pins are symbolically potent and clearly susceptible to imaginative (mis)interpretation.

But the problem doesn't end here. There is serious competition for the limited amount of real estate available for signaling devices on the average suit jacket. The serried ranks of pins are jostling with a rainbow coalition of awareness ribbons (yellow, pink, black, blue, white) representing some undoubtedly worthy cause or other, from breast cancer to AIDS. The wide lapel of the Swinging Sixties may well make a comeback given the army of pins and ribbons seeking public representation. For some of us it's a postmodern version of bird-watching. How many species and varieties of pins can be seen in a week in daylight hours in the Midwest? The March 24, 2003 issue of *The New Yorker* (30) contained a cartoon of "Some New Ribbons" for ambiguous or highly nuanced positions on specific topics, such as: "Support swift, aggressive military action but cannot bring myself to call it war," and "Support colorectal cancer awareness and the Adopt-a-Greyhound program. Oh, and I'm against the war."

Even if this form of marking is not your cup of tea, the social pressure to conform can be extremely hard to resist. Dare you risk being the only celebrity to step onto the stage to accept your Golden Globe without donning the in-vogue pin? The net effect is that everyone troops onstage with the pin and/or ribbon du jour. This quiet coercion mocks free expression and individuality and eviscerates the meaning of the gesture, but to appear pinless or ribbonless these days may result in ostracism. My future as a pariah thus seems assured.

REFERENCE

Schama, S. 2003. "The Unloved American." *The New Yorker* (March 10): 34–39.

NAME DROPPING

"Care to order, guys?" This came from the mouth of a teenage
waitress in a (by Bloomington standards) relatively up-market restaurant. She was addressing yours truly and the late Tom Sebeok,
distinguished professor of semiotics at Indiana University. Tom
was approaching his eightieth birthday; I had passed the half-cen-
tury mark. I glanced at Tom; he chuckled benignly, too kind to say
or do anything. Our server—to use the politically correct label (see
"Wolves in Sheep's Clothing" in this volume)—evidently had no
sense of the inappropriateness of her preferred form of address.
Had we been a couple of twenty-something jocks, I might have
understood, but our demeanor, manners, conversation, and age
were about as far removed from jockdom as possible. I was gob-
smacked, and not for the first or last time. Twelve years on, I am
as appalled as ever by the liberties that total strangers take with
others in this country.

What, I wondered, was wrong with *gentlemen*, a universally understood and socially appropriate term? *Guys* was not just a hope-
lessly inexact noun, given our combined age, but one that implied
a nonexistent degree of familiarity. Perhaps servers believe that su-
perficial familiarity translates into more generous gratuities. Regrettably, familiarity is no longer earned in this country; it is simply
taken for granted by all and sundry. Unlike Bono, Cher, and Sting,
I have two names that I use commonly: "Blaise" and "Cronin."
Call me old-fashioned or self-important, but I expect those who
do not know me or who are mere acquaintances to use the latter,
preferably preceded by a "Mr.," "Dr.," or "Professor." The use of

95

"Blaise" implies some degree of familiarity or intimacy. It is something one works up to, part of a social ritual. God knows how our savoir faire–challenged server would survive in a country like France, where one has to navigate routinely between *tu* and *vous* with all the potential pitfalls. Don't get me wrong, I am not advocating that we adopt the rigid protocols that have characterized the German workplace (bowing and clicking heels in front of Herr Doktor Jahnke or always referring to one's female colleagues as "Frau"), but some controls on excessive familiarity are in order. I do not take kindly to intrusive telemarketers addressing me as "Blaise," nor realtors within ten seconds of a first handshake speaking to me with a familiarity I would not accept from my children. I do not want adolescents or hucksters of any stripe believing that they have the right to speak to me as if I were their friend. I do not want my hairdresser or anyone else hollering out my first name in a salon or other public space. I want a modicum of social respect.

Egalitarianism is all very well, but it should not be used as an excuse for transgressive social behaviors. As it happens, Americans are generally very aware of the need to respect one another's personal space, and the physical separation between two conversing Americans will typically be greater than in most other cultures. Given this well-documented fact (see Edward Hall [1959] on proxemics in general), it is puzzling that there are no comparable constraints operating in the discursive domain—which naturally brings us to the classroom. I was taken aback the first time a student at Indiana University with whom I had never had so much as a passing exchange referred to me as "Blaise" in the lecture theater. In fairness I should confess that during my early career in the U.K., I tried to be hip by allowing my students to call me by my first name, but this resulted in a false sense of friendship that became problematic when contentious disciplinary or grading issues arose. There is, or should be, a gulf separating students from their professors. Of course, things may change when one develops a close working relationship with a doctoral student, but in the classroom I explain that I expect to be addressed properly (i.e., with the appropriate title in front of "Cronin"). I now ask each of my students how they would like to be addressed, and most (actually, all to date) have settled for first names. When I was a student in Dublin, my professors addressed me as "Mr. Cronin." As a teenager it felt somewhat strange to be addressed by one's elders and betters in such fashion, though, to be honest, I rather enjoyed it. But that was then.

Today almost anything goes. Ben Yagoda (2003, B20) recently wrote a piece on contemporary name-calling in academia, noting that the multiplicity of student subcultures on campuses across the nation translates into a variety of local practices. He also highlighted the fact that some female professors, in particular, find a formal title helpful in establishing respectful relationships and dealing with boundary issues. When I visit my dentist or physician, I am happy to address them as doctor (as are most Americans, from what I have observed) in recognition of their professionally validated achievements and status. By the same token, I don't see why my equally hard-earned credentials shouldn't be acknowledged (as, by the way, they would be in the United Kingdom). Senators, judges, and doctors don't have a monopoly on titular propriety. What's good for these professional geese is surely good for the professorial gander.

And now a brief coda. In 1999, I entered into an extended e-mail exchange with the late Robert Merton, one of the preeminent sociologists of the twentieth century. I had drawn upon his work since I was a doctoral student and have always been in awe of his erudition, although we never met. When, during our correspondence, he asked if he could be granted "the privilege of *tutoiement*" and then moved, in the space of a couple of e-mails, from "Dear Dean Cronin" to "Dear Blaise" to "My very dear Blaise," I was touched, but (and this is the pertinent part) I could not bring myself to reciprocate. I found it impossible to address the distinguished octogenarian other than as "Dear Professor Merton" or "Dear RKM." Anything else would have seemed crassly inappropriate. As I reflect on the unconscious discourtesy of the Bloomington server (a trivial instance, I readily concede, of an accelerating national disposition to informality in both personal and social behaviors), I sometimes wonder if I am living in the wrong century.

REFERENCES

Hall, E. T. 1959. *The Silent Language.* Garden City, N.Y.: Anchor Press/Doubleday.

Yagoda, B. 2003. "What Should We Call the Professor?" *Chronicle of Higher Education* (June 13): B20.

MANGLED METAPHORS

It was the Federal Express Christmas card that got me thinking. Not the card itself, you understand, but the inscription: "From the FedEx Family." What family? FedEx is a massive company operating in a cutthroat market with thousands of employees scattered far and wide. Whatever else it may be, it's certainly not a family. That's taking the notion of a family, even a seriously extended family, beyond conventionally or lexically acceptable limits. And, anyway, since when did families send greetings cards signed in type? Just who do the marketing people at FedEx think they are kidding? Presumably, the same people who hear the following words from Katie Couric daily on the *Today Show*: "We'll be right back after these messages." Messages? Messages, my foot! What she means is (paid) advertisements, but, presumably, the truth is too unpalatable for middle-class America to digest that early in the morning.

Does printing the words "FedEx Family" on a bland Christmas card make the recipient feel in any way warm and fuzzy? Do we really imagine that FedEx is, or sees itself as, a family any more than I believe that Indiana University (IU) is one big, happy family? Of course not, but the production of self-deluding and sugary metaphorical usage has begun to spin out of control. I've sat in amazement as intelligent former presidents of IU (and countless other similar institutions) have referred, in both speech and writing, to the IU family. Even my local television station, WTIU, talks straightfacedly about the "membership family." For the record, IU has more than 100,000 faculty, staff, and students all told. Add in living alumni, and you're well past half a million. A family of half a million plus is hard to imagine, even if you're a rabbit. As we all know, university departments, to take a more manageable unit of analysis, are, if the family metaphor must be used, a perfect illustration of the . . . dysfunctional family. Even in the ancient cloisters of Oxbridge colleges, the dons are anything but family-like in their behaviors, as C. P. Snow (1951) described so vividly. Compare a university with a corporation, a holding company, a collectivity, if you must, but certainly not with a family.

What lies behind this penchant for the reassuring metaphor— "messages" for "ads"; "FedEx Family" for "hordes of employees"; "family" for "sprawling university community"? Where has truth in advertising gone? Why do intelligent individuals and organizations talk down to us? Why do they debase language, and why does no one seem to care? We've seen this pattern before, when military brass and Pentagon spokespersons refer to human casualties as "collateral damage" and successful air attacks are labeled "surgical strikes," as if one were talking about an episode of *ER* rather than bloodshed in Bosnia. We may not like this pasteurization of the unpalatable (other choice examples from the military's expanding lexicon include "kill ratios," "kinetic targeting," and "precision-engagement capability"), but the logic is easy to grasp, and the practice has been exhaustively analyzed by sociolinguists and communication theorists. Geoffrey Nunberg (2003, 58) noted recently that "the language of war is becoming more business-like," (business speak, in turn, has long relished military analogies) with tanks and plans being relabeled "assets." Sanitized speech has become a depressing norm. Handicapped individuals are repackaged as "alternatively abled," as if such alliterative rewriting of reality might somehow make one feel better about oneself (see "Wolves in Sheep's Clothing" in this volume).

Again, one has to ask, who's fooling whom? Why the "IU family"? Why package something that is a million miles from most people's definition of a family in such a silly fashion? Family implies blood relations, proximity, tight kinship structures, and a shared identity. The answer is simple: Since family members look out for one another, members of the hyperextended IU family will look out for their own. And how will they do that? By making gifts and creating endowments to support successive generations. In that respect, IU is, of course, no different from any other institution of higher education in this country; it's just a shame they all resort to the same threadbare metaphor to get their messages across. More to the point, it's insulting to those of us who must listen to such twaddle from individuals, colleagues in some cases, who should know better.

REFERENCES

Nunberg, G. 2003. "Fighting a War with Words." *Fortune* (March 3): 58.
Snow, C. P. 1951. *The Masters*. London: Macmillan.

THE LANGUAGE OF LEARNING

It's easy to scoff, but sometimes it's absolutely necessary. The new managerialism that has taken root so aggressively in the world of British higher education invites parody at the very least. And nowhere is this better illustrated than in its contortionist use of the English language and its predilection for marketing mantras throughout what these days is known grimly as "the sector." The *Times Higher Education Supplement* (*THES*) is the U.K. equivalent of the *Chronicle of Higher Education*, and, as I've discovered of late, its job announcement pages are at once a source of great mirth and sadness. What follows provides merely a flavor of all that is wrong in the groves of academe; life is too short to conduct anything approximating a systematic survey or analysis of the root causes; for that, I recommend *The New Idea of a University* (Maskell and Robinson 2001) and *Universities in the Marketplace* (Bok 2003) for a British and American perspective, respectively. I clipped a few position announcements from a couple of recent *THES* issues for closer inspection, and here's what I found.

The headhunting firm of Heidrick & Struggles has been hired to find a vice chancellor and chief executive (president, in U.S. parlance) for the University of Luton. Before going any further, it should be pointed out that the University of Luton is among the lowest ranking of all U.K. universities; indeed, it has a singularly unfortunate knack of attracting less-than-flattering media attention, as regular readers of *THES* well know. At the top of the display advertisement under "University of Luton," we find the words "Education that Works." This is a peculiar phase in that it implies that some other institutions may be in the business of providing education that *doesn't* work. Would one expect anything less than "education that works" from a university, moreover from one which boasts, as Luton does without blushing, "considerable achievements?" The successful candidate will be expected to provide the institution with "clear and charismatic leadership" for what promises to be "truly a unique opportunity." Oh, dearie me!

The University of the West of England (UWE) is a self-described "**learning**-intensive university" (note the word "learning" in bold type). UWE sets itself apart from the rest of the pack by choosing "to do teaching **and** research, not teaching **or** research" (and, yes, both "and" and "or" are in bold). This approach will enable UWE to become (all in bold this time) "**a new kind of first class university**." One can hardly wait to enroll in UWE's creative writing program.

Across the Irish Sea, another relatively new institution, Dublin City University (DCU), is looking for nothing less than a "Vice President for Learning Innovation," an imposing-sounding position for which, it turns out, a mere associate professor would be eligible. The lucky individual will be "responsible for the formulation of DCU's teaching and learning strategy and for championing learning innovation." Unless I'm sadly mistaken, Bologna, Oxford, Cambridge, Paris, and Harvard Universities, to mention but a few, have managed to maintain the highest academic standards for centuries without resorting to such dubious strategies and puffed-up language.

At the University of Surrey, the search is on for an "Academic Liaison Manager within Information Services." By way of explanation, Information Services "is a multi-stranded service," and what is needed is an "experienced and proactive manager," preferably one with "success in target driven team management." Frankly, I have absolutely no idea whether I am eligible to apply since I haven't a clue what they're talking about.

But these four specimens pale in comparison to the jumbo-sized advertisement placed by Riley Consulting on behalf of the University of East London (UEL—another of the thirty-three polytechnic ducklings which were metamorphosed into university swans in 1992). The UEL ad kicks off with a quotation from Charles Darwin no less: "It is not the strongest of the species that survive, nor the most intelligent, but the ones most responsive to change." And guess which university is responsive to change. You've got it! "Our diverse and innovative learning environment has seen UEL become one of the most vibrant and forward thinking Universities in the Capital (*sic*). We're acting as a dynamic force behind the economic and cultural regeneration of the Thames gateway region and our new Docklands campus has won world-wide acclaim." And almost as an afterthought, we're told that UEL has been "ranked among the top ten post-1992 universities for research," which, I might add, is hardly cause to break out the bubbly.

The university is "looking for people who share our vision as we enter an exciting period of change and roll out our new management structure." Here, in one advertisement, is the finest collection of nonce words you're likely to find: "innovative learning environment," "forward thinking," "vibrant," "dynamic force," "world-wide acclaim," "exciting period of change," and "roll out our new management structure." Somehow I don't think I'll be encouraging my children to apply to the University of East London.

To a greater or lesser extent, these five institutions (and they are not alone in this) are guilty of cloaking their aspirations in a form of verbiage that is as misleading as it is vulgar. Quite simply, their self-presentations make one wince. How is it that universities, of all organizations, can so flagrantly debase the English language; do they really, for one moment, imagine that we don't see through their multistranded, gossamer claims?

REFERENCES

Bok, D. 2003. *Universities in the Marketplace: The Commercialization of Higher Education.* Princeton, N.J.: Princeton University Press.

Maskell, D., and I. Robinson. 2001. *The New Idea of a University.* London: Haven Books.

WEASEL WORDS

"Charles is a decent cove; just the chap for the job." Time was when a ringing endorsement like this would have landed you a plum position. By the same token, a succinct, "Wouldn't touch Smithers with a barge pole," was enough to have one's application consigned instantly to the trash can, irrespective of one's actual capabilities and experience. Things have both improved and deteriorated since then. The power of the old boys' network is not quite what it once was, and talent and accomplishments will, on a good day, beat out the old school tie. But transparency in recruiting and promotion has come at a cost. Voluminous curricula vitae, from high school up, now itemize every micro-accomplishment, and the design-conscious CV routinely comes with a self-aggrandizing cover letter, which unabashedly tells the unfortunate reader why the writer is indubitably the best-qualified candidate on the planet for the position.

These days, it seems as if every graduating student has been tutored in the arid art of CV preparation, and bullet points come as if from a Gatling gun. The result is a hail of look-alike products wrapped in "me too" prose and pomposity. What must employers think? Some in Libraryland are plainly not happy (LaGuardia and Tallent 2002). For me, the plasticity of the language and the preening self-presentation are the hardest to digest. But it gets worse when we move up the food chain to the professorate. Here, as we all know, self-promotion is a way of life, and we regularly and unblushingly remind the world just how distinguished we are. Some curricula vitae are as long as a novella, with sections and subhead-

107

ings—dynamically updated testimonies to our prodigious talents
and accomplishments in the hypercompetitive world of the academy. And then there are the letters of application, sometimes two,
sometimes three pages long. A few are almost appropriately modest, but most are as puffed up as a goose waiting to be transubstan-
tiated into pâté de foie gras. Then there is my favorite triptych design: Why me? Why here? Why now? This is seriously proactive
self-promotion. In case members of the reviewing committee can't
quite figure out why you're the bee's knees, you do their work for
them.

But the whole exercise veers off into topsy-turvydom when we
get to the battery of accompanying letters of reference. These un-
solicited paeans to one's character and diligence are both cloying
and formulaic to a degree that demands parody (they are, in effect,
solicited, but this is conveniently overlooked). They gush, ooze,
and dribble false sincerity, resorting to a hackneyed vocabulary of
superlatives. It's an epistolary inflationary trend worthy of the Wei-
mar Republic. Every one of us is a disciplinary leader who can only
be described as outstanding, exceptional, pioneering, excellent,
and rigorous. Commenting on his experience as a Harvard professor who read students' recommendation letters, Harvey Mansfield
(2003, B8) explains, "stock analysts and traveling salesmen could
learn their craft from such letters today."

Where, I sometimes wonder, are the mediocre folks—life's lieu-
tenants, the ordinary, the average, the soon-to-be has-been, yester-
day's man, the maverick, the kinda-out-there young turk? It's Lake
Woebegone to the power of three. The problem with these letters
is twofold: first, we get our buddies to write them (so every compli-
ment should automatically be discounted) and, second, no reference letter writer would dare speak ill of the candidate/applicant
or make even the slightest qualifying remark for fear of litigation.
Many universities inform letter writers and referees that the person about whom they're writing may read their reference. Liability
has throttled honesty in a process that is manifestly bankrupt, yet it

continues to consume an unconscionable amount of the academy's time. But only a few questioning voices are heard from under the dead weight of the po-faced prose, and a lot of very intelligent people continue to play a very unintelligent game; a game that, ultimately, undermines the system. One voice of reason is that of the noted economist, Deirdre McCloskey (2002, B14), who suggests:

> Colleges should make their own decisions about tenure and promotion, doing the homework required and using the outside world's information. . . . The only correct procedure for assessing scholarship in hiring or promotion is for the responsible body to read the candidate's work and discuss its intellectual quality with immediate colleagues in a context of believably disinterested assessments from the outside.

But that's not the whole story; a good friend of mine recently wrote a somewhat critical evaluation of a candidate seeking promotion to full professor and was roundly upbraided by the candidate's colleague who seemed to believe, genuinely, that those invited to comment should only do so if their comments were positive. This view, based on recent anecdotal evidence, seems to be gaining ascendancy. What a house of cards we are creating!

The apogee of this self-delusional system is, of course, the promotion and tenure dossier. Think of a milk crate; no, think of two, three, even four milk crates bulging with tediously documented evidence designed to prove one's capacity to be granted tenure and/or promotion. Imagine the sight every spring on the nation's campuses as crates of boxed futures are hauled from office to office to be examined, dissected, and, finally, archived. Recently, I was confronted with a four-crater. How, in the name of all that is good and holy, I wondered, could it require four crates of material to demonstrate that the candidate was qualified? One is reminded over and over again of the Shakespearean adage, "the lady doth protest too much."

Padding is no substitute for substance, and the seasoned reviewer will bypass all flimflam to focus on what matters most in a research university—namely, evidence that a scholar's work has been subjected to peer review and, moreover, has had some kind of meaningful impact. There are time-honored ways in which this can be demonstrated, without resorting to the milk crate game. But the crates keep on coming, the prose becomes more clotted, and the futility of the entire exercise slowly saps the will of the good souls who remain. And the suits seem to neither notice nor care.

REFERENCES

LaGuardia, C., and E. Tallent. 2002. "Interviewing: Beware Blogging Blunders." *Library Journal* 127, no. 15:42.

McCloskey, D. 2002. "The Random Insanity of Letters of Recommendation." *Chronicle of Higher Education* (March 1): B14–15.

Mansfield, H. 2003. "How Harvard Compromised its Virtue." *Chronicle of Higher Education* (February 21): B7–8.

Card Games

Originally published February 2003
This article was coauthored with my colleague Yvonne Rog-
ers, whose contributions are duly acknowledged.

There is some dispute as to the origins of the visiting card, but by
the eighteenth century it was in widespread use among certain
strata of society. This was notably the case in France, where the
design of the humble card had, in fact, become a minor art form.
A century later, the visiting card was an indispensable accoutre-
ment of the socially conscious lady or gentleman, from the salons
of Paris to the drawing rooms of Boston. The calling card was considered a mere piece of paper at one's peril, according to the 1881
edition of the etiquette manual *Our Deportment* (www.lahacal
.org/gentleman/cards.html): "To the unrefined and underbred, the
visiting card is but a trifling bit of paper; but to the cultured disci-
ple of social law, it conveys a subtle and unmistakable intelligence.
Its texture, style of engraving, and even the hour of its leaving
combine to place the stranger, whose name it bears, in a pleasant
or a disagreeable attitude." It is worth noting, in passing, that the
British Museum's Department of Prints and Drawings houses a
collection of visiting cards, a testimony to the card's sociohistorical
and aesthetic significance.

An elaborate web of rules and conventions developed around
the visiting card and its use, and both sender and receiver understood the governing etiquette. For example, a hand-deliverd card
for the lady of the house should have one corner turned down

(each corner representing a different statement) while a card in an envelope delivered in response to an in-person call indicated that visiting between the parties should cease. In polite society, a business card could not be proffered in lieu of a visiting card; their purposes were quite distinct, though doctors, lawyers, and a few other privileged occupational groups were permitted to use one card for both social and professional purposes. A married woman was expected to include her husband's name and title, but she could not use her own first name unless she was widowed. A married woman calling formally on another married woman would leave three cards: one of her own and two of her husband's, one each for her friend and the friend's spouse. Today, purists and minimalists may still insist on name and (mailing) address only— engraved, naturally, in black on white paper—but, increasingly, telephone, pager, and e-mail information feature as well. As the panoply of telecommunications gadgetry grows, that list will surely expand.

In the course of the twentieth century, the social visiting card was largely eclipsed by the business card, and today no self-respecting business person (or academic, for that matter) would travel without a sheaf of cards. The card exchange ritual has been universally and enthusiastically adopted in the business world and beyond. Although the protocol of using visiting and business cards today is simpler than it was in Victorian times, there is still considerable cultural variation in the exchange rituals (what is acceptable in Japan may not be in Korea or China, for instance). The typical business card contains more information than a calling card and is much less understated. The elements may include full name, academic and/or professional qualifications, title (and rank), company/ organization name, complete address, various phone and fax numbers, e-mail address, corporate website and personal homepage URLs, and organizational logo. In some cases, the information may also be printed on the reverse in a second language. During the 1980s, photographs were added to the array of discretionary elements, along with full-color design. Additionally, one had the option of paper or plastic cards of variable sizes (including double-folded)—prepunched, if necessary, for inclusion in a Rolodex.

By the end of the twentieth century, the business card had evolved into a sometimes dandyish and often information-rich advertising tool. In so doing, it lost the subtle and nuanced communicative role associated with the visiting card. The social intelligence—to which the initiated were privy—afforded by the various physical manifestations of the visiting card has been replaced by the singular need to provide contact information alongside a more blatant form of branding and institutional/company promotion, now ubiquitously accepted as the business card's main purpose.

Several authors have considered the role of genre in understanding emerging digital environments (Bates and Lu 1997; Vaughan and Dillon 1998; Yates and Sumner 1997) but, as far as we can tell, no one has examined the visiting card's evolution and role in digital environments. This overlooked genre and its digital mutations (e.g., signature files, vCards) deserve closer scrutiny.

Signature files are typically five to six lines in length, approximately sixty characters wide, and include some or all of the following: name, organization, contact address, phone number(s), URL(s), e-mail address(es), brief product description, company motto, quotation, and/or ASCII (text) art. Many of these elements can be found on business cards, though the closest approximation to text art would presumably be a logotype. Conventions and expectations, of course, vary across contexts and domains, and many websites offer guidance on appropriate practice. By way of illustration, the VirtualXML Netiquette Guidelines (www.cmlconsulting .com/vxml/concourse/notices/netiquette.html) are explicit: "Please ensure that email signature files do not conspicuously promote your product or service. Excessively large signatures (greater than four lines) that promote products or services will be treated as advertisement."

The actual netiquette for using signatures, however, is in sharp contrast to the subtle conventions that applied to the use of visiting cards. While most people initially used the signature function in the way for which it was designed—to provide contact details akin to those of the business card—a growing trend is evident, particularly among professionals, including some of our peers, to use their signatures to represent their achievements and highlight selected scholarly activities. In so doing, the signature has expanded beyond its original identifier function into an executive summary or bio capsule of the sender. Such self-promotion is typically employed by those of high status in their community as a way of informing others about the importance of their achievements—a practice not yet adopted with business cards.

This is an example of commingling genres, where the signature file is appropriated to provide both contact information and further salient details about the particular individual. The ability to easily edit and update a signature file encourages this dual role: additional material can be added or the order of elements can be rearranged to reflect priority. For example, a URL for a newly published book by the sender, or a forthcoming conference organized by that individual, may be placed just under the sender's contact details to highlight the latest achievement. It is reasonable to assume that digital developments will accelerate further change and experimentation: As Yates and Sumner note, there has been "a loss of fixity with the onset of easily editable digital documents and digital communications" (1997, 3). This loss can have a destabilizing (or liberating) effect on the development and use of established communicative genres in digital contexts.

Being able to easily modify one's signature file provides scope for customization. Indeed, individuals frequently have more than one version. Of course customization is not unheard of in the physical realm; some individuals have more than one business card because of cultural or other differences in groups with whom they interact. However, the customization afforded by virtual signatures is more *personalization*. In addition to adding and changing the

order of additional material, users may "fold" various forms of con-
textual information into their signature files, such as clickable Web
links, inviting the recipient to virtually "visit" them and learn more
on their Web pages. Another trend has been to add a quote from
some eminent writer, composer, or artist who epitomizes one's
philosophy of life and implies a level of intellectual prowess, for
example:

> *"True success will always have the transitory character of improvi-*
> *sation, but also—and don't underestimate this—its freshness"*
> *—G. Mahler*

Parallels between business cards and signature files have been
made. The Real Estate Information NETwork (www.reinet.com/
library/computers/file33.htm) asserts that the signature file "is the
on-line equivalent of a business card." Elsewhere it is noted that
"signature files serve the same purpose [as business cards] in the
online business" and are, in fact, "mini-ads" (akkabay.com/market
ing/sigfile.html). But the signature file has, in some respects, di-
verged in its purpose from the business card. It has the feel of a
hybrid genre, combining such aspects of the calling card as personal data interchange, with the business letterhead (www.web
novice.com/sig_files.htm). As already noted, the number and diversity of elements (from e-mail address to the individual's photograph) carried by the typical business card have increased over
time. A similar trend is apparent with the signature file. The "va-
nilla" version will include key contact information but little else.
At the other extreme, signature files can contain apothegms, offers
to the reader (e.g., visit our website and receive a free . . .), and
comic drawings (ASCII art). A full-blown signature file goes well
beyond the original function of a business card (to introduce and
succinctly profile oneself, and also to act as an after-the-fact surrogate for the giver). In short, the visiting card has metamorphosed
into an interactive marketing device. The signature file remains—

notions of hybridity notwithstanding—a recognizable instance of the visiting card genre

The cycle of genre evolution may continue with the advent of vCards (www.imc.org/pdi/). The vCard is an electronic business card (the business card metaphor is an integral aspect of the associated marketing effort). The vCard is also the name of the underlying industry specification. A vCard is sent as an e-mail attachment or as a link on a Web page. It can include images, audio content, logos, and geo-positioning information as well as text—a significant advance over signature files and printed business cards. Recipients of a vCard are able to add (simply by dragging and dropping in some case) the sender's information into their electronic address book, provided it is vCard-compliant. The vCard can be thought of as an animated interactive version of the classic visiting/business card. However, it is not welcome everywhere; plain text signature fields are deemed preferable to vCard attachments on Usenet (see www.cs.tut.fi/~jkorpela/usenet/vcard.html).

One of the possible reasons for the unpopularity of vCards is that they are designed as "attachments," sent indiscriminately and repeatedly with each e mail. Whereas it is seen as a faux pas to give more than one business card to the same person on separate meetings (since such an act signals that the person does not discriminate among acquaintances in the way that is conventionally accepted in face-to-face networking), such etiquette does not presently exist with vCards. Instead, they are used in the same way as signatures, attached to every e-mail by default. The vCard shouldn't be confused with other superficially similar signaling genres, such as the I-card (also known as an identity or smart card), which can function, for example, as both a library card and a debit card, or with a "Gaydar" device, a portable, interactive ice-breaker for gay men and women (www.usatoday.com/life/cyber/tech/review/crg942.htm). Although the I-card has some format similarities with the visiting/business card, essentially it is a tool that supports private rather than public or social interaction.

Gaydar, though an artifact for identifying kindred spirits, so to speak, is not functionally equivalent to a visiting card. It is simply a rudimentary screening device.

For the vCard to become a more versatile mode of communication, changes to its design would be required. For example, e-mail software could be designed to recognize recipients who have been previously sent a vCard; the software could notify the sender, allowing him or her to decide whether to resend the vCard. Additionally, like signatures, the user should be able to create a range of alternative vCards, allowing subsequent ones to be shorter, updated, or more "personal," signifying to the recipient that the sender is aware of the relationship/bond between them. Enabling more sensitive means of communication would overcome some of the problems associated with the current generation of vCards. Better communication could also bring back some of the subtle intelligence and pleasure associated with the delivering and receiving of visiting cards, making them a distinct genre not to be confused with the business card and its marketing/branding function. That said, one doesn't want to overdo the analogy since it is unclear whether a vCard etiquette has emerged, or whether senders and receivers have a common appreciation of the underlying conventions, as was the case with Victorian visiting cards.

Shifting from the professional/business world to the social sphere, it is interesting to note that the Victorian visiting card in its "pure" form is experiencing a cyber renaissance. In addition to signature files and vCards, attempts have been made to move the classic visiting card from the print to the digital world. Many websites (e.g., www.victorianflair.net/CallingCards.html) offer a variety of calling cards that can be displayed on website guest books, on bulletin boards, or used as e-mail attachments. There is also a "Web ring" for calling cards (gerdesdesign.com/callingcards/). This trend suggests that the blurring distinction between the social calling card and the more aggressively functional business card, as instantiated in both signature files and vCards, may be reestablished.

The visiting card is experiencing a digital revival, both in pure (neo-Victorian) and emergent form. The signature file and its potential successor, the vCard, may or may not be uniquely digital genres—they are arguably and recognizably descendants of the visiting card we associate with the eighteenth and nineteenth centuries—but they show how the structural, linguistic, and graphic properties of an established communicative genre can be adapted to a new medium. For the digital versions to acquire or move beyond the sophisticated use associated with Victorian visiting cards, however, requires designers to provide more scope by which to customize and personalize vCards. First, users need to become aware of the subtle and different forms of messaging that vCards potentially have to offer, and, secondly, users should be able to create their own set of cards with coded and symbolic meanings—as with the folding of the Victorian paper card—understandable to others in the ways intended. Just as the signature file has evolved to serve multiple functions beyond what was originally intended, so, too, may the vCard expand by revisiting its communicative roots.

REFERENCES

Bates, M. J., and S. Lu. 1997. "An Exploratory Profile of Personal Homepages: Content, Design, Metaphors." *Online & CDRom Review* 21:331–40.

Vaughan, M., and A. Dillon. 1998. "The Role of Genre in Shaping Our Understanding of Digital Documents." Pp. 559–66 in *Proceedings of the 61st Annual Meeting of the American Society for Information Science.* Medford, N.J.: Information Today.

Yates, S. J., and T. R. Sumner. 1997. "Digital Genres and the New Burden of Fixity." Pp. 3–12 in *Proceedings of the Hawaiian Conference on System Sciences (HICCS 30),* Special Track on Genres in Digital Documents, VI.

VIRTUAL VENTING

I blog, therefore I am. These days, Hyde Park Corner is only a few HTML tags away. The Web has become the universal soapbox. No voice need be unheard; no whine denied oxygen. It's the fusion of vanity publishing and the bully pulpit. Every idea, no matter now trite or crazy, can see the light of digital day. There's a new lexicon: blogs, blogging, bloggers, and live journaling. Weblogs are sprouting like primroses in spring. The so-called blogosphere now comprises an estimated 500,000 weblogs.

A weblog is a site that provides online commentary, personal ruminations, and links to other sites. Some are like personal journals or diaries, "podiums for bush-league blowhards" (Wolcott 2002, 77); others are topically focused and offer more or less mature commentary, essays, analysis, or criticism. Rebecca Blood has provided a pocket history on her website (www.rebeccablood.net/ essays/weblog_history.html), noting that weblogs provide a useful filtering function; readers come to them knowing that the Web has been "pre-surfed." For a sense of what's on offer, visit Weblogs. com, which lists hundreds of examples of this emerging journalistic subgenre.

Some of the weblogs I have looked at are bland if well intentioned; many are downright puerile and embarrassingly egotistical. Generally speaking, these are not folk who have kissed the Blarney Stone or graduated *summa cum laude* from either a journalism or creative writing program. What's most startling (well, of course, it isn't in the least startling) is that these pundits imagine that their digital dribblings might be of interest to someone. In terms of de-

119

sign, weblogs run the gamut, ranging from the manifestly amateur-
ish to the edgily sophisticated. The owners, a.k.a. commentators or
editors (you can hire an editor to create content if you're stuck for
words, and there are powerful template builders for the techni-
cally challenged [Hammersley 2003]), presumably crave attention,
or at least want to share their thoughts on life and the universe (or
a slice of it) with others of similar outlook—a mutual reinforce-
ment of views. As Cass Sunstein puts it, the new communication
technologies are "dramatically increasing people's ability to hear
echoes of their own voices" (2001, 49). Others disagree and prefer
to see blogging as an expression of pluralism and dialogic democ-
racy in action.

   In a sense, the average blogger is not very different from an op-
ed columnist, an editorial writer, or a jotting Jeremiah. As you can
imagine, instead of writing for *Library Journal* and publishing the
odd book with Scarecrow Press, I realize that I could take my not-
so-humble opinions and pontifications directly to the Web, and,
quite conceivably, attract a larger audience, hook even more eyeballs, and become Libraryland's answer to my fellow expatriate
Andrew Sullivan (www.andrewsullivan.com). Now there's a blogger par excellence, a first-rate journalist and budding public intellectual who offers informed commentary on politics, culture, ho-
mosexuality, and other issues along with links, letters, interviews
(read the one with Camille Paglia), and book reviews. His site is
an attractive, well-designed, and information-rich weblog that
boasts a lot of pageviews per month. Mr. Sullivan is no free-enter-
prise slouch; he unashamedly invites $20 + subscriptions from
devotees to help with site maintenance.

   The weblog is becoming the twenty-first-century weapon of
choice for the maverick, ideologue, social activist, concerned citizen, revolutionary, and egomaniac. It's also for academics. Apparently, blogs are "sprouting like mushrooms" in the groves of academe (Glenn 2003, A14). Some are very popular, some are
somewhat popular, and many are unpopular; think of it in terms

of a power law. InstaPundit.com, authored by Glenn Reynolds, a University of Tennessee law professor, averages 100,000 hits daily, while The Volokh Conspiracy (volokh.com/), a twelve-person group blog (primus inter pares is Eugene Volokh, a UCLA law professor), attracts 8,000 hits per day.

According to a recent report, bloggers have been credited with bringing down former Senate majority leader Trent Lott by keeping his racially insensitive remarks alive until the mainstream media broadcast them. Blogging has been touted as the instantiation of participatory journalism and an example of nanopublishing (Frauenfelder 2003). Imagine if Martin Luther had had access to the Web. No need to nail tracts to wooden church doors. Instead, kindred spirits would have flocked to his electronic portal. Or would they? That, of course, is the main question. If we all become bloggers, who'll have time to read all the blogs? Some bloggers will reign supreme; most will be virtually invisible. After all, the Web is often spoken of as a winner-takes-all market, although that's an oversimplification (Huberman 2001). In the attention economy, there's only so much time to go around; for every Andrew Sullivan, they'll be scores, if not hundreds, of hopefuls who merit or attract little attention, which is scarcely surprising—many bloggers are windbags, only a few know their onions.

Those heavy on providing links (with brief commentary) bring to mind classical technological gatekeepers; individuals who thrive on sharing information informally and for whom peer recognition itself is the reward (Cronin 1982). The role performed by these organizational pollinators and boundary spanners is similar to that performed by the best of the blogger population. Other bloggers have a rather more entrepreneurial motivation. Weblogs are potentially a very effective branding device, where the blogger is the product. What better way to initiate a cult following than by becoming a particular domain's weblog of choice, whether cryptic crosswords, Humphrey Bogart movies, or library shelving systems? Find a topic that's blogless and aggressively develop a presence as the chosen cyber gatekeeper and commentator for that clearly defined segment, and eyeballs will surely roll your way.

But it's not quite that simple. You're going to have to refresh your content, links, and commentary on a regular basis if your viewers are going to return to your site. Stickiness that translates into repeat visits and informal recommendations is the secret to success in this game. That means uploading fresh material while you're vacationing on Martha's Vineyard, or, alternatively, having an *atelier* of assistant bloggers who can be relied upon to keep the blog alive in your absence. Human nature being what it is, I expect that many of the early enthusiasts for this particular form of self-expression will quickly drift away, that others will be relegated to the status of a footnote in the history of digital marginalia, and that only a few will be in it for anything approximating a long haul. It's pretty obvious that serious blogging calls for a hefty investment of time, effort, and imagination. Successful bloggers will know that a dynamically updated weblog amounts to a cyber ball and chain wrapped around virtual ankles, and only the most dogged will persist, once the initial flush has faded.

REFERENCES

Cronin, B. 1982. "Invisible Colleges and Information Transfer." *Journal of Documentation* 38, no. 3:212–36.

Frauenfelder, M. 2003. "Nick Denton, Blog Mogul." *Wired* 5:30.

Glenn, D. 2003. "Scholars Who Blog." *Chronicle of Higher Education* (June 6): A14–16.

Hammersley, B. 2003. "Bloggers Tool Up." *Guardian* (March 24): 25.

Huberman, B. A. 2001. *The Laws of the Web: Patterns in the Ecology of Information*. Cambridge, Mass.: MIT Press.

Sunstein, C. 2001. *republic.com*. Princeton, N.J.: Princeton University Press.

Wolcott, J. 2002. "Blog Nation." *Business 2.0* (May): 77–79.

BURSTING INTO PRINT

First, the good news: any fool can get published. Now, the bad news: any fool can get published. In the academic library world, there is considerable pressure to publish, and we are drowning in a sea of numbingly mediocre papers posing as meaningful research. I guess it's an attempt to sustain the nineteenth-century Germanic model of the scholar-librarian. Regrettably, the practice is effectively institutionalized in many universities through policies that grant academic/faculty status to librarians. The quid pro quo is that librarians are expected to crank out would-be scholarly articles for publication in professional journals. I have already expressed my views on the subject of faculty status for librarians in *Pulp Friction* (Cronin 2003), and I shan't air them again. In any case, the reality is that some academic librarians both want and are required to publish, so how does one come to grips with the scholarly literature? The suggestions that follow are based on a talk I was unable to give (because of the combined effects of SARS and budget cuts on attendance) at a Library Administration and Management Association (LAMA) conference in Toronto in mid-2003, entitled "Create Knowledge, Not Nonsense: Taking Responsibility for Our Literature." They are aimed at neophytes.

Let me begin with a few basic tips on how to read "the literature": (1) Don't be put off by jargon; in the right hands and under the right conditions it promotes effective communication. (2) Be suspicious of any sentence that contains two or more of the following: "hegemony," "problematized," "privileging," "intertextualizing," or "habitus." (3) Parse the text; some professors write literal nonsense, but they write it deceptively well. Don't let them pull the wool over your eyes. (4) Just because an author cites Lacan, Foucault, Bourdieu, Derrida, et al. doesn't mean that he is to be taken seriously. (5) A paper's quality is not proportional to the size of its bibliography. (6) If an author hasn't cited the fundamental literature, the wheel (minus the spokes) is probably being reinvented, or, worse, plagiarism is being perpetrated.

Next are several suggestions on how to critically engage texts: (1) Read the literature of your field closely; it's guilty until proven innocent. (2) Remember that research without theory is like Boeuf Bourguignon without beef. (3) Deconstruct the author's argument; carefully examine the methods, assumptions, data analysis, interpretation, and generalizations. (4) What is unsaid? What's missing from the frame? Is there evidence of experimenter effect, ideological bias, black box sampling/statistical analysis, etc.? (5) Are the methods used in the research appropriate to the problem under investigation? (6) Are the conclusions warranted by the evidence presented in the study? (7) Is the work an example of cookie-cutter research or original thinking?

And now I offer a few basic suggestions on how to test or challenge the claims being made: (1) Remember that powerful inferential statistics are no substitute for weak data. (2) Correlation is not causation. (3) Learn the errors of your ways (Type I and Type II). (4) There's something called ecological validity—what happens in the lab may not happen in vivo (the real world). (5) The biggest sample is not necessarily the best. (6) Life is inherently messy and complex; univariate analysis is, well, not. (7) Qualitative is not the opposite of quantitative; look for ways to combine investigative methods. (8) Be open-minded, trust your gut, and be tolerant of mixed approaches.

So how do you get started? (1) Stick to a domain that you know. (2) Identify key publications and authors before embarking on your project. (3) Check who has recently been citing important papers (forward chaining using citation databases). (4) Read the *An-*

nual Review of Information Science and Technology (you'd expect me to say that, wouldn't you?) and other important review articles to get your bearings in the field and avoid duplication. (5) Look for (interesting) gaps in prior work, questions that have been over-looked, approaches that haven't been tried, etc. (6) Frame the issue or problem clearly and locate your approach in the relevant body of theory. (7) Develop working hypotheses, design some pre-liminary probes, use an exploratory or convenience sample, and run a pilot survey before launching the study proper. (8) Review and reevaluate as you work; don't be procedurally, methodologi-cally, or conceptually inflexible. (9) Establish whether any proven test instruments exist that you might be able to use. Try not to re-invent the wheel.

Finally, how are you going to ensure that you are influential? In the end, quality will triumph, but you may be able to increase your odds to attract readers. (1) Think collaboration and coauthorship. Research shows that multiauthored papers are statistically more likely to be cited. (2) Seek out faculty partners as mentors, guides, or coworkers. (3) Exploit local institutional resources, such as op-portunities for grant funding, colleagues, and reputation. (4) As-certain the impact factors and rejection rates of particular journals. (5) Match your research topic with the target journal's scope. (6) Use "trusted assessors" to review your work, that is, those col-leagues near and far whose judgment you respect. It's a great way of detecting errors and infelicities before sending the paper off to editors and referees. (7) Consider the attractions of self-publishing or posting your work on the Web or including it in a working paper series. (8) Beware of "physics envy"; library science is what it is, and there's no point in trying to dress up disciplinary mutton as spring lamb.

REFERENCE

Cronin, B. 2003. *Pulp Friction*. Lanham, Md.: Scarecrow Press.

HOLDING THE CENTER

What follows is an impressionistic assessment of the major centripetal and centrifugal forces reshaping the landscape of information studies education. The focus is North America, although some of the trends find their echo in other contexts. I consider the health of the field in terms of its (1) critical mass, (2) coherence, (3) credibility, and (4) creativity, and I speculate on its likely future constitution. Some of these issues have been addressed in the final report of *KALIPER*, the *Kellogg–ALISE Information Professionals and Education Reform Report* (www.alise.org/nondiscuss/kaliper_final.pdf), the purpose of which was to analyze, using the case-study method, recent curricular change in Library and Information Science (LIS) education. In short, this study found a "vibrant, dynamic, changing field." The issue I want to consider is whether the field in question, vibrant though it may be, can persist as a coherent and credible whole or whether centrifugal forces will bring about conceptual fragmentation resulting in the eventual dissolution of the domain.

It has become rather fashionable to analyze information studies education ecologically. Stuart Sutton and Nancy Van House's brace of "Panda Syndrome" papers (1996; 1999) attracted attention. They observed—correctly and uncontentiously—that "survival of LIS education does not necessarily mean the survival of current programs, and certainly does not mean their survival in their current forms. It means survival of the knowledge base, approaches, values, practices, and tools which must be applied to new problem areas" (Sutton and Van House 1996, 145). However, structural change of this kind had been anticipated for some time: "As far as the USA is concerned, we can expect rolling closures and emergent stratification, with consolidation at the top end of the market. Some programs will continue, but in a different host environment and in different forms" (Cronin 1992, 201). In the decade since those words were written, we have witnessed precisely these kinds of developments, most notably, perhaps, progressive stratification within the population of North American information studies schools. And as Sutton and Van House imply, there has been a revalorization of curricular staples such as classification, indexing, and citation analysis in an age of metadata, ontologies, and hyperlinks.

The *KALIPER* study is not entirely off-beam in its optimistic assessment of the LIS field: it indeed captures the mood of the moment. Talk of library school closures have faded and been replaced by a much more optimistic outlook among most faculty. New programs are being launched (especially at the undergraduate level, in information studies or some variant thereof), and approximately a dozen schools (e.g., Drexel, Illinois, South Carolina) now offer master's degrees via distance learning. Moreover, the job prospects for graduates remain fairly strong. And there are other indicators which suggest that the field is finding its research feet: impressionistically, more information studies faculty are now bidding for and securing grants from agencies such as the National Science Foundation (NSF)—and not just in connection with the multiagency, multimillion-dollar Digital Library Initiatives (www.dli2.nsf.gov/). Another heartening sign is the (admittedly modest) increase in the number of endowed chairs (e.g., Dominican, McGill, UCLA) and named professorships (e.g., Chapel Hill, Indiana) held by information studies faculty. That said, the LIS field has experienced its own highly acrimonious culture wars, provoked, in part, by perceived strategic drift and loss of professional values.

By the late 1990s, the former library school at the University of California, Berkeley, the nation's premier public research institution, had transmogrified into a school of information management and systems, no longer providing library science education. Berkeley does not offer the Master of Library Science (MLS), nor does it feature in the Association for Library and Information Science Education (ALISE) directory or the organization's annual statistical compilation. It has finally and definitively left the club. This was not a case of program closure but a strategic (and institutionally mandated) repositioning. Berkeley may have been the first defector, but it will surely not be the last. Will the traditional club, hang together? Or will the forces that are pulling some of the larger, more academically prestigious schools away from the center result in further membership depletion and, ultimately, domain identity loss? Of course, a rejoinder might be that the residual (smaller) group would perforce have a stronger identity, albeit one achieved at the expense of prominence.

It's hard not to feel that the club will break up, for two reasons: First, the glue that traditionally held the club together (the MLS degree) is increasingly just one element among an expanding range of both graduate and undergraduate offerings. Schools like Chapel Hill and Indiana offer Master of Information Science (MIS) degrees alongside the traditional MLS. In revenue (and other) terms, the MLS is no longer the lynchpin it once was. Second, a number of schools in the ALISE troupe (e.g., Drexel, Michigan, Indiana, Pittsburgh, Washington) are currently talking to and meeting with other schools that are broadly interested in information technology and its applications. A new discourse space has been fashioned in the last year or so, bringing together deans and directors of computer science, information technology, information systems, and information science programs with progressively converging interests. This fledgling formation, known as the Information Technology Deans' Council, emerged from under the wing of the Computing Research Association (CRA, www.cra.org/) in July 2000, following an inaugural gathering at Snowbird, Utah. A growing band of ALISE members is now represented in this loose alignment of information technology and computing schools, and it will be revealing to see whether the (historical) LIS schools within this group persist with dual organizational membership or forsake the old (ALISE) in favor of the new (CRA). On top of this, a group of LIS deans and directors has recently engaged in discussions about creating yet another body that would represent the interests of so-called information schools.

Alongside the more or less established population of information studies schools (almost, though not quite, coextensive with the institutional membership of ALISE) is a cluster of new entrants to the evolving space, notable among them Penn State's School of Information Sciences and Technology and Indiana University's School of Informatics. Both of these are interdisciplinary start-ups with strong institutional support and major funding behind them. They are not reengineered library schools (like Berkeley or Michigan), but green field developments designed to take advantage of the growing market demand for graduates with grounded and well-rounded appreciation of information technology and its social ramifications. At Penn State, the new school fills a clear void, as that institution had no library school program. At Indiana, the new School of Informatics coexists with the long-established School of Library and Information Science. At Berkeley, the School of Information Management and Systems has simply replaced the library school. At present, a variety of developmental models are being tested across the nation, and the experimentation seems likely to continue.

As the information studies domain expands, and as new entrants take up position in the enlarged (and, admittedly, still fuzzy) space, traditional LIS programs will be threatened. At the very least, they run the risk of being overshadowed by the new wave of informatics and information studies/science/systems programs being established to meet both labor market and academic administrators' expectations. It seems highly likely that some of the more robust LIS schools will progressively abandon the center in favor of the periphery as, over time, it becomes a new center of intellectual gravity. In such a scenario, the residual heartland population will be a significantly weakened body with diminished academic credibility.

The trends sketched here bode ill for the more traditionally defined LIS programs, as these are deficient in both critical mass and academic credibility. That is to say, they lack political capital, are vocationally rather than scholastically focused in their endeavors, and exhibit little creative thinking about their imminent plight. The upshot may be a graphically stratified arrangement of the kind predicted some years ago (Cronin 1995, 46): "Two, if not three, distinct populations of schools will emerge over the next few years; pace setters which decouple almost entirely from the LIS heartland; would-be boundary spanners, balanced delicately between the old and new worlds; and a *Lumpenproletariat* of schools lacking the resources, imagination, and will to reposition themselves for the twenty-first century." Even if this terminology is not to everyone's liking, the underlying argument is hard to rebut.

A number of LIS schools have changed name in the last decade. Of the fifty-six schools listed on the ALISE website (www.alise.org/), twelve do not have the word "library" in their titles. Many have "information" plus "science" or "studies" alone or in combination with "library science." However, the University of Michigan, which renamed its library school "School of Information" (no qualifying "management," "science," "systems," or "studies" required), may have started a trend, anticipated perhaps by Neil Postman, who cleverly chronicled the post-Enlightenment emergence of "the idea of context-free information" (1999, 87). For good measure, the University of Washington recently rebaptised its library school, somewhat hubristically, as "*The* Information School." Presumably, the rest of us will have to be content with being *an* information school, like the recently rebadged LIS program at the University of Texas at Austin.

In some cases, these changes in nomenclature are largely cosmetic in that they do not herald major internal transformations (e.g., Wisconsin-Milwaukee); in others (e.g., Michigan), they signal a significant shift in terms of organizational structure, asset concentration, and academic orientation. In any event, such actions invariably provoke the wrath of heartland librarians who perceive the dropping of the L-word as an abandonment of professional values and core curricular concerns. Some schools consciously attempt to achieve a balance between centrism and peripheral engagement. The Illinois website's welcome statement (alexia.lis. uiuc.edu/gslis/school/index.html) contains the following mini manifesto: "The School's faculty believes strongly that librarianship and newly emerging related fields must be held together to prevent libraries from becoming obsolete and other fields from being unconcerned about issues of access, privacy, and service." This stance is what is meant by "holding the center" in the title of this paper.

Library school closures, a topic of great concern particularly during the 1980s, have been few and far between of late. The domain (defined in terms of institutions with programs accredited by the ALA) has exhibited striking stability since then. Instead of elimination, programs are more likely to be enveloped or combined into new, presumptively stronger, configurations. UCLA's LIS program lost its autonomy and is now a component part of the School of Education and Information Studies, while the University of Western Ontario's library science program has been incorporated into a Faculty of Information and Media Studies. Most recently, Buffalo merged its communications and LIS departments to create a School of Informatics. This, it should be noted, is not a new phenomenon. Rutgers pioneered the multidepartmental model in the 1980s, and, one imagines, the same generic arguments about resource rationalization, administrative efficiencies, and academic synergies are being invoked by today's academic administrators to justify current reorganizations.

Several of the high-profile information studies schools (e.g., Michigan, Syracuse) are noticeably pulling away from the rest of the pack. Regardless of the battery of indicators used (e.g., student numbers, faculty productivity, endowment income, external research funding), the gap between leaders and laggards is widening. Resource disparities inevitably translate into a scholastic gulf between the elite and the rest, which accreditation—often (and mistakenly) viewed as an equalizer—does nothing to reduce. Typically, the pacesetters can mobilize additional institutional resources to upscale their activities and launch strategic initiatives, both in terms of teaching and research. The best the remainder can hope for is incremental base budget growth and, occasionally, opportunistic funding from a benign institutional parent, extramural agency, or benefactor. Such developments have dramatically raised the costs of "staying in play" for many schools and departments.

Accreditation is a blunt instrument for protecting space, and it is no guarantee of academic quality, according to the American Council of Trustees and Alumni (Leef 2003). The interventions of the ALA's Committee on Accreditation (COA) have had the effect of constricting creativity and preventing the domain from extending its "jurisdictional control," to use Abbott's (1988) term. Following the introduction of the COA's 1992 Standards of Accreditation of Master's Programs in Library and Information Studies (www.ala.org/alaorg/oa/stanindx.html), schools found that they could no longer assume that the re-accreditation period would be seven years. Variable renewal became a disquieting fact of life, and some of the top-ranking schools in the nation (e.g., Indiana, Michigan, Syracuse) were granted renewal periods of less than seven years, while manifestly weaker institutions received the full seven years.

The lack of transparency in the COA's accrediting regime, notably the vagueness of the criteria and their application, became a matter of public concern and rancor, which may just have helped precipitate a set of proposals for changes in prevailing practice (www.ala.org/congress/accredtf) made by an ALA task force. This committee's main proposals were that the ALA's monopoly on accreditation should end and that a federated body—a separate 501(c)3 organization—should be established to conduct accreditation reviews. The new entity would include other relevant professional groups, such as the American Society for Information Science and Technology and the American Records Management Association in addition to the ALA. Fortunately, the LIS deans, to their credit, deemed this to be a nonstarter.

Ironically, the restrictive effects of a narrow professional accreditation regime on a field (such as information studies) exhibiting strong expansionist tendencies has been the ceding of peripheral space to nimbler and more intellectually creative programs from cognate disciplines. The price of clinging to the center has resulted in claim-staking opportunities. Potential territorial loss of this kind may matter little to atavistic groups like the COA, but, in the age of "post-professionalism" (Cronin and Davenport 1988), it can ultimately have a deleterious effect upon the ability of LIS programs to build and sustain academic credibility within their host institutions or to attract the best and brightest students.

There is, of course, a sense in which none of this actually matters. Scholars and researchers, whose principal loyalty, more often than not, is to their discipline rather than their parent institution or some professional body, will inevitably continue to collaborate with distributed colleagues irrespective of whether their peers' schools are labeled centrist or peripheral, domain insiders or outsiders. These sociocognitive links will transcend formal institutional labels and status indicators. However, from the standpoint of organizations such as the ALA, it will become painfully clear that the premier information studies programs, scholastically speaking, are no longer card-carrying members of the LIS fold. The net effect will be an even weaker critical mass and, consequently, diminished institutional and professional legitimacy. This, over time, will trigger an irreversible downward spiral with serious recruiting and image implications for the library profession nationwide. To appropriate a metaphor, which Taylor (1979) originally used more than twenty tears ago, we are witnessing a shift from a Ptolemaic to a Copernican information universe. To put it another way, traditional LIS programs are being decentered as the study of information (which now includes topic areas such as human-computer interaction, knowledge management, information architecture, social informatics, and information economics) becomes an attractive proposition for both start-ups and established academic programs in related domains.

While some may lament the progressive marginalization which LIS programs seem likely to suffer (and the associated weakening of both institutional and professional credibility which such a trend engenders), the good news is that the academic study of information will move from strength to strength as new institutional structures and circuitry (e.g., the CRA initiative mentioned earlier) emerge to fill the gap. Of course, the refashioning of the landscape may not result in a clear bi- or even trifurcation; it is conceivable, at the very least, that a robust population of boundary spanning schools could emerge. Such a "broad church" grouping, defined in terms of catholicity, critical mass, harmony, and synergy seeking (Cronin 1992, 199–200), which might include, for the sake of argument, programs like Indiana, Illinois, and Texas-Austin, would strive to maintain links between (at the risk of oversimplifying) the worlds of ALISE and the CRA. If so, it might just be possible to hold the center while colonization of the periphery continues apace. But the odds are long, as these hybrids will undoubtedly experience increasing difficulty in maintaining coherence of identity, image, and purpose.

REFERENCES

Abbott, A. 1988. *The System of Professions: An Essay on the Division of Expert Labor.* Chicago: Chicago University Press.

Cronin, B. 1992. "Information Science in the International Arena." *Aslib Proceedings* 44, no. 4:195–202.

―――. 1995. "Shibboleth and Substance in North American Library and Information Science Education." *Libri* 45, no. 1:45–63.

Cronin, B., and E. Davenport. 1988. *Post-professionalism: Transforming the Information Heartland.* London: Taylor Graham.

Leef, G. C. 2003. "Accreditation is No Guarantee of Academic Quality." *Chronicle of Higher Education* (April 4): B17.

Postman, N. 1999. *Building a Bridge to the 18th Century: How the Past Can Improve Our Future.* New York: Vintage.

Sutton, S. A., and N. A. Van House. 1996. "The Panda Syndrome: An Ecology of LIS Education." *Journal of Education for Library and Information Science* 37, no. 2:131–47.

―――. 1999. "The Panda Syndrome II: Innovation, Discontinuous Change, and LIS Education." *Journal of Education for Library and Information Science* 40, no. 4:247–62.

Taylor, R. S. 1979. "Reminiscing About the Future. Professional Education and the Information Environment." *Library Journal* 104, no. 16:1871–75.

HONORIS CAUSA

Originally published winter 2002–03

Dame Edith Sitwell was unequivocal. "Fools," she once wrote to John Gielgud, "are made doctors by other fools in other universities, but no fool has ever been given an Hon. D.Litt. by Oxford." No fool she; her Oxonian gong was awarded in 1951, an occasion which she proclaimed to be "the proudest and happiest moment of my life." Oxford has been conferring honorary doctorates for more than 500 years, the first having been granted in either 1478 or 1479, and one marvels at Dame Edith's unshakable trust in the ancient university's quality control mechanisms over the centuries. Parenthetically, one wonders what the vice-chancellors of Leeds and Durham Universities, the first to honor Sitwell in this fashion, would have felt had they been privy to her correspondence with the distinguished thespian.

The poet John Skelton was granted this honor by Cambridge in 1493, the first on record for the upstart in the Fens. Since then, many distinguished names have wended their way to the twin pinnacles of British higher education to receive what Mark Twain, honored by Oxford with a Doctor of Letters (D.Litt.), called these "unearned finds"—of which, by the way, he had a respectable clutch. Twain, like Sitwell, took the invitation from the city of dreaming spires most seriously, inconveniently crossing the Atlantic to receive his D.Litt. in person. Perhaps Dr. Sitwell—as she very much liked to be addressed, according to Victoria Glendinning (1981) in her biography—was not alone in her assessment of the degree's worth.

Commencement and other academic rituals were exported from the Old Country to the Colonies, and Harvard was the first college to award an honorary doctorate to its then president, Increase Mather, who received a Doctor of Sacred Theology (S.T.D.) in 1692. Today, the S.T.D. is something of a collector's item, with the Doctor of Laws (LL.D.) and Doctor of Letters (D.Litt.) being among the more commonly awarded honorifics. By 1775 Harvard had awarded only five honorary doctorates, all, it must be said, to Harvard graduates, gentlemen *d'un certain âge*. In the years ahead, the pace would quicken, but, astonishingly, it was not until 1955 that the institution conferred an honorary doctorate on a woman. Helen Keller may hold the distinction of being Harvard's first female honoree, but she was by no means the first woman to be so honored by an Ivy League institution. Mary Emma Woolley, in the vanguard of Brown University's female graduates, retired from the presidency of Mount Holyoke College in 1937 having amassed no fewer than twenty honorary degrees from institutions nationwide, including an honorary doctorate from her alma mater. In the main, however, women were overlooked.

Yale conferred its first honorary doctorate, a Doctor of Medicine (M.D.), in 1723. Later New Haven notables included John F. Kennedy, who remarked famously: "Now I have the best of all possible worlds, a Yale degree and a Harvard education." Princeton's first was an LL.D. in 1769, while Dartmouth gave a Doctor of Divinity (D.D.) in 1773. In the City of Brotherly Love, Philadelphia, the University of Pennsylvania awarded its first honorary doctorate in 1782, and a year later conferred an LL.D. on none other than George Washington. The practice of granting honorary doctorates to the Great and the Good (G&G) is not universal; some notable institutions (among them, I believe, Cornell, MIT, Rice, Stanford, Vassar, and Virginia) have pretty much managed to resist the temptation, while others (Princeton, Harvard, and Yale, to name but three) have each awarded several thousand over the years. The one-time record, though, may have been set by Columbia, which awarded 134 in 1929 alone. This annus mirabilis happened to be the university's 175th anniversary.

Thanks to one Stephen Edward Epler (1943), we know a quite a bit about the social history of the honorary doctorate in the United States. His book (based on a Ph.D. thesis completed at Columbia University) provides a painstaking and statistically informed account of American honorifics from the earliest days to 1938. It is a little gem, dated to be sure, but packed with fact, anecdote, and insight. As far as I can ascertain, this is the only scholarly monograph devoted to a subject that is otherwise superficially, if frequently, treated in newspaper and magazine stories, as an hour or two searching on *LexisNexis* will reveal. One may also stumble across the occasional opinion piece or chapter on the subject of honorary degrees (e.g., Freedman 2002; Freiherr 1979), but the challenging task of updating Epler's pioneer survey has yet to be undertaken.

Given the remarkable post–World War II growth in higher education, it is a safe bet that the trends described by Epler have risen in the intervening decades. Unfortunately, there are no reliable figures on the number of honorary doctorates awarded annually in the United States; apparently, the American Council on Education ceased counting in 1973, and no one has assumed responsibility since then, but a guesstimate of 5,000 to 10,000 per year is probably in the ballpark. By any reckoning, that's an awful lot of greatness and goodness to recognize, except, of course, that it's no longer the case—as if, indeed, it ever were—that these awards are reserved exclusively for members of the G&G club. It also means, according to my conservative, back-of-the envelope calculations, that at any given moment there are some 100 to 150,000 honorary doctors in circulation in the United States alone, which scarcely suggests selectivity. Compare this with the number of Nobel laureates alive at any given moment. In short, the honorary doctorate has fallen victim to academic hyperinflation. On both sides of the Atlantic, there is ample evidence, historically and presently, of how abused this venerable system of academic preferment has become.

"If," as Epler notes in his conclusions, "honorary degrees had been given only to Newtons, Darwins, and Einsteins, the prestige of the honorary degree system at the present time would be unquestioned." He might have added, "and if they had been conferred by the Harvards and Princetons of this world." However, if doctorates are being doled out in the thousands every year, not all can be going to paragons of science, scholarship, and statecraft. For every Newton and Darwin on the roll call of honor, there's a pride of lesser souls—pop stars, sporting heroes, CEOs, politicians. These "muttonheads in mortarboards," to quote a nameless New York editor, populate commencement platforms, displacing deserving dons and progressively devaluing the degree. It's Gresham's law in the groves of academe. And for every Ivy League school, there is a slew of minor colleges keen to get in on the act, which merely underscores the importance of securing one's gong from a blue-chip institution. Breeding *is* branding in this game. Nothing new in all of this, of course: Abraham Lincoln was granted an honorary doctorate in 1860 by Knox College, "a young institution just struggling for reputation," according to Orville Brown, a trusted and longtime friend of the honoree, who wrote Lincoln of the good news. Abe still accepted.

Whilst the rot may have set in, we've not quite reached the point where either Princeton or Cambridge University is likely to wrap Britney Spears in scarlet robes any day soon. Cambridge's criteria include "conspicuous merit" or "distinction" in the case of foreigners. Also admissible are members of the royal family, though, given the public antics of Queen Elizabeth II's progeny of late, this policy may warrant review. Princeton, no mean school, has granted Bob Dylan, no mean troubadour, a Doctor of Music (D.Mus.) degree, one up, in every sense, from Billy Joel's Southampton College award. Even St. Andrews, one of the world's oldest universities, couldn't resist the temptation to grant honorary doctorates to two golfers, Colin Montgomerie and Seve Ballesteros, when the Open championship came to the old town a few years back. Par for the course these days, methinks.

Come Trinity term, kings and commoners, not to mention a growing caravan of ex-presidents from Clinton to Gorbachev, converges on our nation's campuses. Resplendent in their medieval attire, they process gravely through quadrangles, neo-gothic and neon-lit, before finally moving center stage for their sub-Warholian moment of unearned academic glory. Brief citations are read—in Latin, if you're very lucky. Most often the recipient is silent, an immobile peacock, whose sole requirement is to doff his cap, don his hood, and clasp the parchment before withdrawing to make room for the next in line.

Nobility is always a safe bet at such occasions, whether King Harald of Norway or the Prince of Wales (with, at last count, fifteen to his credit). Icons such as Nelson Mandela will be surefire successes, though the competition to attract top-of-the-line luminaries can be fierce. Mandela disappointed the two universities in Leeds by declining their joint offer of an honorary degree. The University of Leeds was particularly galled since it had previously named a newly discovered fragment of matter the Mandela Particle. (The discovery was later found to be a mistake caused by faulty equipment.) To rub salt into Yorkshire wounds, Mandela subsequently accepted an honorary Doctor of Laws degree jointly from the University of Sydney and the University of Technology, Sydney, adding to his impressive tally of more than forty. During 1996, he had a stellar streak, bagging a novena from British universities, which, naturally, included a brace from Oxbridge.

But the A-list is short; for every Mandela there are a dozen Don ("American Pie") McLeans, Nicolas Cages, or Wayne Gretzkys only too willing to be hooded. In recent years, my own institution has awarded honorary doctorates to, among others, Jane Pauley, a TV news anchor, and John Mellencamp, a determinedly mediocre

rock singer. Does anyone seriously believe that either of these individuals, or individuals of comparable stature, would have been
similarly honored by Harvard or Oxford? Bottom feeding seems to
be the order of the day, but this won't come as a complete surprise
to those who recall that Kermit (the puppet frog) delivered the
1996 commencement address at Southampton College. Without
question, this wheeze attracted media attention, but what kind of
public relations fillip was Southampton seeking?

Honorary doctorates are typically awarded to a small number of
individuals at the same time, which creates opportunities for artful
combinations—rather like arranging place settings for dinner
guests. Yale, for instance, recently awarded doctorates to Julie Andrews and Alan Greenspan, an inspired juxtaposing of songstress
and sphinx. The "his" and "hers" approach also has its attractions.
Ryerson University (Toronto) cleverly awarded honorary doctorates to both Nelson Mandela and his wife, Graça Machel, while
south of the border, Ted Turner and (estranged) wife Jane Fonda
picked up their degrees à deux from Emerson College in Boston.
(They weren't estranged when they accepted the invitations.)
Even if you're six feet under, it's possible to nab an honorary doctorate, a case in point being the degree awarded posthumously to
General Murtala Muhammad by the Bayero University, Kano,
twenty-five years after his death.

In a break with tradition, the University of East Anglia in the
United Kingdom gave an honorary doctorate to the charity Comic
Relief in recognition of its fundraising activities. One may sympa-
thize with the symbolism of the gesture, but the idea of corporate
honorifics within this particular realm makes little sense. There are
many other awards that would be more fitting for such purposes.
The same holds for what might be termed human interest cases,
such as that of Doris Haddock, a nonagenarian, who walked from
California to Washington, D.C., to promote campaign finance reform. This sterling effort was deemed worthy of an honorary doctorate by Emerson University. By this token, it's high time some-

one offered a posthumous gong to the character in David Lynch's touching movie *The Straight Story*, who doggedly drove his lawn-mower across middle America to visit his ailing brother. Which of our schools will step up to the plate?

There are no reliable data on the distribution of honorary doctorates by class of recipient, although of late it seems as if scholars have become a distinct minority, with donors (established and prospective), politicians, and that truly protean category, celebrities, accounting for the bulk of the awards. Epler's figures for the United States from the seventeenth century to 1928 show that law, business and the military combined accounted for a mere 10 percent of all degrees conferred, with the category "academic and professional" garnering almost 50 percent of the awards. These days, corporate leaders are routinely recipients of honorary doctorates; the disgraced cosmopolite, Robert Maxwell, harvested his internationally—from Aberdeen, Moscow, and New York Universities. In fact, some CEOs seem to appear at commencement ceremonies almost as often as they do on the covers of *Fortune* or *BusinessWeek*.

Of course, corporations are also frequent donors, and successful CEOs are not bashful about paying through the nose to have their names affixed to chairs, professorships, scholarships, buildings, and facilities of every variety. The Regius Professorship of Moral and Pastoral Theology at Oxford has a certain ring to it, but I'm not altogether sure that the same can be said of the Taco Bell Distinguished Professor of Hotel and Restaurant Administration at Washington State University, to say nothing of the Enron Chair in Risk Management in the Jesse H. Jones Graduate School of Management at Rice University. *Autres temps, autres moeurs*. The Kelley School of Business at Indiana University got its name (and some $20 + million for student scholarships) from the philanthropic founder of the Steak 'n Shake restaurant chain. However, he didn't "do an Enron" and endow a named chair after his restaurants; for such small mercies we are indeed grateful. Gifts of this magnitude are now staggeringly commonplace, which explains why Harvard's endowment exceeds the gross domestic product (GDP) of more than a few African nations. Without such largesse, the history of higher education in the United States would have been quite a different story.

But *some* donors do have expectations (*Timeo Danaos et dona ferentes*), and one very effective and efficient way of satisfying their appetite for recognition is to grant them honorary doctorates. And even if donors don't have expectations, rest assured some universities will be only too pleased to reward such generosity with an honorary degree. When McGill University in Canada conferred a doctorate on scientist cum entrepreneur Richard Tomlinson, it was in return for a $64 million gift to his alma mater: "We're not going to pretend that it's for anything else. This is our way of saying 'thank you,'" stated Principal Bernard Shapiro, unapologetically. Dr. Tomlinson—a career academic at McGill—was not trying to buy a second doctorate, but even if he had been, $64 million would have been an astronomical price to pay for the privilege of writing Sc.D. (Hon.) after one's name. The problem really lies at the other end of the spectrum, where merely showing up and delivering a twenty-minute commencement address can fulfill postnominal fantasies. This practice is to be condemned unreservedly, and one can only hope that highly visible individuals who are offered this kind of inducement to visit Podunk College will follow John F. Kennedy's reported example by accepting the invitation to speak while graciously declining the offer of a degree.

Until recently, tracking the arrival of plutocrats and parvenus at High Table was a fairly easy matter; the names appeared week-in and week-out in the "Glittering Prizes" section of the *Times Higher Education Supplement* (*THES*). That the University of Westminster should have awarded Peter Boiszot, founder and chairman of Pizza Express, an honorary doctorate would be nothing more than lamentably commonplace for devotees of the *THES*. This wave of honorees brings new values and behaviors to the fore.

Some insist on being addressed as "Doctor," blind to, or casually dismissive of convention in this regard. They would do well to heed Dr. Samuel C. Gipp, Th.D. (*sic*): "Academically, an honorary doctorate is like an 'honorary black belt' in karate. Wear it around the house, but don't try to *use* it or you'll get killed!" Others, like David Hockney and Archbishop Trevor Huddleston, bring a dash of eccentricity to the proceedings: the popular painter accepted his Leeds doctorate wearing a pair of red corduroy slippers, while the Red Bishop celebrated his Oxford prize with a clenched fist salute. The ever-engaging painter of pools has also announced that he'll not be accepting any more honorary doctorates. "This is it," he told *The Guardian*, "it might sound grand to be a four times doctor, but you cannot write out prescriptions for your own drugs on this."

Do Sheryl Crow (successful recording artist), J. K. Rowling (best-selling author), Tiger Woods (golfing god), and George Best (legendary soccer player) really need honorary doctorates? In their respective worlds, they are high-profile successes, and their enormous public acclaim has been matched by pecuniary gain. They have garnered plaudits, prizes, medals, and sundry other tributes during their careers, so why is it necessary to acknowledge their resolutely nonacademic achievements with an academic honor? As has been pointed out on more than a few occasions by dyspeptic observers of current trends, we give musicians Grammys and film actors Oscars, but we certainly wouldn't expect Stephen Hawking or Edward Said's latest books to result in either Grammy or Oscar nominations. Why not, as was suggested in a *Daily Mail* article some years ago, simply award athletes and others of that ilk an honorary "blue," the traditional signifier of sporting distinction within British university life (see "Coach Class in Academia" in this volume)? By granting honorary doctorates willy-nilly, universities have made a monumental judgment error. The resultant lampoonery is both self-inflicted and entirely justified.

Despite the inflationary spiral, some genuinely distinguished professors can still be spotted at the podium when the goodies are being dished out. The statistician C. R. Rao has twenty-four honorary doctorates from fifteen countries. Catherine Stimpson of New York University has already collected a dozen in the course of her career, while Noam Chomsky, one of the United States' most visible and vociferous public intellectuals and highly cited scholars of all time, received an honorary doctorate, in the space of about a week, from the University of Cambridge for his foundational work in linguistics and another from Amherst College for his political activism.

We tend not to be surprised that honorary doctorates, like Nobel laureates, are often awarded to graying eminences. These garlands are typically reserved for capstone achievements and outstanding lifetime accomplishments. Of course, exceptions to the rule can be found. In 1784 Harvard conferred a doctorate on the 27-year-old General Lafayette, while in 1928 Wisconsin awarded an LL.D. to the high-flying Charles Lindbergh, aged 26. As far as I can tell, Lindbergh, along with classical pianist André Watts, is the youngest recipient of an honorary doctorate on record. Another youthful phenomenon is Linus Torvalds, creator of the Linux open-source operating system, who, at age 29, was similarly honored in 1999 by Stockholm University. However, honorary doctorates are not (yet) a topic entry in the *Guinness Books of World Records*, so my data should be treated with caution.

The rarified world of the honorary doctorate provides a telling illustration of the Matthew Effect: "For unto every one that hath shall be given, and he shall have abundance." The Dalai Lama can muster a credible number (eight plus a first prize for Humanity from the Sartorius Foundation, which must be worth something). Prince Charles may have a tidy score, but in his case it's effectively a birthright. In the early part of the twentieth century, General John Pershing received a dozen honorary doctorates in a three-year period from both British and American universities, a particularly fecund spell by any standard, and all the more impressive when one considers that the conferring institutions included Oxford, Cambridge, Harvard, and Yale—not just quantity, but quality. A word of advice to members of the armed services: a good war will work wonders for your chances of academic ennoblement.

To date, the playwriting Czech president Václav Havel has accumulated almost forty, an eye-catching achievement. The late Barbara Jordan, an African American politician and educator, managed a lifetime score of thirty-one. Presidents Dwight Eisenhower and Herbert Hoover had more than seventy and eighty, respectively, currently putting their South African counterpart, Nelson Mandela, in the shade. But even Hoover, with his eighty-four or eighty-five degrees, can't claim the top spot. That honor, as far as I can tell, goes to Rev. Theodore M. Hesburgh, president emeritus of the University of Notre Dame, whose Web page proudly notes "his 147 (as of 6-8-01) honorary degrees." It's not clear whether all of these are doctorates, but it would be quite unseemly to nitpick. Father Hesburgh is in a class apart and has set an intimidating, perhaps unsurpassable, benchmark for all would-be collectors of honorifics. Most of us in academe will never be honored thus; a few will receive the call but once, and only an infinitesimal number will hit double digits. This is what statisticians mean by a power law of cumulative advantage.

At what point do the G&G become blasé: a baker's dozen, a score, more? Or, do they become addicted, fearful that the flow of public encomia will dry up one day? Perhaps, among this superelite, keeping up with the Joneses has been redefined in terms of symbolic capital formation. That said, some heavyweight collectors are also highly discriminating: a decade or more ago, the 1981 chemistry Nobel prizewinner, Ronald Hoffmann, told *The Scientist* that "every year I turn down and I accept some." He won't accept an honorary degree if he feels an institution is using him "for publicity, to get prestige for themselves." Three cheers for Hoffmann!

Not everyone, though, is bowled over by the prospect of a glittering prize from the institutions of learning. Former presidents Cleveland and McKinley, the philosopher Herbert Spencer, and South African Betsie Verwoerd all reportedly declined the honor. The reasons vary. If you've already got one from, say, Berkeley or Edinburgh, you may not want to devalue it by taking another from (perish the thought) a minor state college or, in the United Kingdom, a former polytechnic. Who, in their right mind, would want to accept an honorary doctorate from BoJo—the Bob Jones University? To which the retort is "someone like the Rev. Ian Paisley." In academia, as in life generally, the company you keep matters. A polite refusal may be the best course of action, particularly if there's a risk you'll find yourself seated on a dais with a hyperventilating frog or caterwauling clergyman.

Unsurprisingly, there seems to be an inverse relationship between an institution's prestige in the academic firmament and its enthusiasm for dispensing honorary doctorates. A quick perusal of the "Glittering Prizes" column over the past couple of years is enough to demonstrate the cavalier commitment of Britain's "new universities" in honoring individuals of exemplary ordinariness, such that the University of Idaho's awarding of an LL.D. to a restaurateur who featured "the genuine Idaho baked potato" seems almost laudable. Illustrative of the trend, though not an especially egregious example, is the University of Salford's honorary doctorate to Leonard Steinberg. Apparently, Steinberg has helped make "gambling popular and respectable," thereby allowing the university to develop a reputation as a national center for training graduates for the gambling industry—a textbook instance of public-private sector interaction or an example of moneylenders in the Temple of Learning, depending on your point of view. What, pray, would Cardinal John Henry Newman make of all this?

Let us assume that not all honorary degrees are awarded in order to achieve transsectoral synergies of the Salfordian variety. And let us further assume that they are not always a quid pro quo—for a seven-figure gift or prospect thereof. In some cases the motivation may be disinterested; nothing more or less than a genuine expression of esteem from one's academic peers, as when the University of Nottingham awarded an honorary doctorate, in absentia, to the sociologist Harold Garfinkel. This is an instance of gift giving without the expectation of reciprocation, which is not the same as saying that high-mindedness precludes the possibility of some benefit accruing to the awarding institution at some point in the future.

But for every selfless award there is, rest assured, one that is manifestly self-serving, whether the institutional aim is to curry political favor, attract donations, or bask in reflected glory, such as when a celebrity—president, pundit, pop star—rolls into town. Despite administrators' protestations, it is obvious that honorary doctorates, like indulgences in times bygone, can be bought, though not always cheaply—a view, incidentally, that pops up with some frequency in the Australian press. According to the *Sydney Morning Herald*, the University of Sydney is doing the right thing by tightening its honorary degree system and setting a proper example for the rest of the pack. "No more trophy patrons" seems to be the mantra du jour down under, but will reformists hold sway in the face of continuing cutbacks in public funding for higher education?

This is not to say that all university presidents are guilty of traducing a time-honored practice; some institutions have rigorous nomination and evaluation criteria (Harvard being a case in point) and will doughtily resist external pressures to grant so-and-so the desired honor. Which, of course, brings us to Margaret Thatcher and the rebuke conferred on her by her old university. The antipathy of Oxford's dons, scientists in particular, to the then prime minister's higher education policies, was such that they did the unthinkable: they broke with tradition by refusing to grant her the honorary doctorate that was hers by virtue of the office she held—*trahison des clercs*, according to *The Economist*. In an historic vote, 738 to 319, Mrs. Thatcher's nomination for an honorary doctorate was rejected, and one can only speculate, as Anthony Kenny does in his autobiography *A Life in Oxford* (1997), what effect this very public and considered slight had on the evolution of higher education policy in the United Kingdom.

The Oxford brouhaha is an illustration of how politics and academe can collide, but it's hardly unique. There was opposition to President Charles Taylor of Liberia's honorary degree granted by Morehouse College, while a campaign was launched against the Chinese University of Hong Kong's conferment of a doctorate on Lee Kuan Yew, the Singaporean Senior Minister. Back in the United States, six demonstrators were arrested at the University of Florida for protesting against General Norman Schwarzkopf's honorary doctorate in public service. Even President Number 43's honorary degree from his alma mater, Yale University, generated hostility in some quarters, despite this being something of a Bush family tradition.

Evidently, and hearteningly, not everyone feels that the significance of an honorary doctorate has been irredeemably devalued or that the situation is beyond redemption. It's also comforting to know that some recipients are possessed of sufficient social conscience to return their degrees when the awarding institution fails to live up to expectation . In 1985 the poet Judith Wright returned hers in disgust when the University of Queensland awarded an honorary LL.D. to the sitting premier Sir Jon Bjelke-Petersen. The same thing can also happen in reverse. In 2001 the National Agrarian University in Peru stripped deposed President Alberto Fujimori of his honorary doctorate for "ethical reasons." This was a doubly stinging rebuke since Fujimori had been the university's rector at one time.

It is abundantly clear that not all recipients of honorary doctorates are alike or singled out for similar reasons. On the one hand, we have legitimate members of the G&G club—scholars of distinction, statesmen, and grandees from the fine and performing arts worlds (such as James Watson, Mary Robinson, Leonard Bernstein, Dario Fo, Robert Motherwell), who are neither cynical nor in any way dismissive of the tradition. Indeed, Mark Twain wore his Oxford D.Litt. robes to the marriage of his daughter Clara, an engagingly idiosyncratic expression of what the degree meant to him. Gertrude Elion, 1988 Nobel prizewinner in medicine, whose honorary doctorate tally rose to double digits, was quoted as saying that the honor "is comparable with getting elected to the National Academy." The problem is not scholars' perceptions of the significance of an honorary degree qua degree—most are tickled pink to be publicly acclaimed by their peers in this fashion—but with institutionally sanctioned abuses of the reward system resulting from the progressive corporatization of higher education.

On the other hand, we have a motley and aggressively populist crew drawn from the worlds of mass media, sports, local politics, and the enterprise culture (think Gloria Estefan, Tom Selleck, Jack Nicklaus, Bill Gates). This is a crass division, but you get my point. By all means, let our universities continue to bestow the traditional honorary degrees (D.Litt., Sc.D., D.Mus., etc.) on the A-list as appropriate, but—and this is not an original suggestion—for the others it is time to institute a new breed of honorary doctorate (D.Hon. has been proposed), or even a university fellowship or medal, which is reserved for those categories of accomplishment that have no scholastic component to them. The pop stars, dot.com millionaires, and sporting gods will still have their day in the sun, but the integrity of the traditional degree will not be compromised.

REFERENCES

Epler, S. E. 1943. *Honorary Degrees: A Survey of Their Use and Abuse.* Washington, D.C.: American Council on Public Affairs.

Freedman, J. O. 2002. "An Honor to a Degree." *Chronicle of Higher Education* (May 24): B10.

Freiherr, G. T. 1979. "Is There an Honorary Doctor in the House?" *Change* 11, no. 4:22–25.

Glendinning, V. 1981. *Edith Sitwell: A Unicorn Among Lions*. London: Weidenfeld and Nicholson.

Kenny, A. 1997. *A Life in Oxford*. London: John Murray.

RESIDENT ALIEN

Recently I received a gold-embossed envelope, which contained an invitation to attend a fundraising dinner with former President and Mrs. George H. W. Bush in Washington, D.C. No doubt many people receive such invitations, but I was both perplexed and angered. Below is the reply I didn't send to the 41st President of the United States, which explains why I feel the way I do.

President George Herbert Walker Bush
P.O. Box 96221
Washington, D.C. 20077

Dear President Bush,

Thank you for the invitation to the 2003 President's Dinner in Washington, D.C. Regrettably, I must decline. Permit me to say why I am unable to attend.

First, and this should not come as a surprise to you, I am unaccustomed to writing a $2,500 check for my supper. Such a figure may not cause the average oil industry executive to blink, but I can assure you that it induces rapid eye movement in even a relatively well-remunerated academic. Second, I can only assume that you want my company because the Republican Party wants my vote. And it is precisely here that we have a problem.

You may not be aware, but I am not a U.S. citizen. I hail from the motherland of your predecessors Kennedy and Reagan. I am, in the parlance of the federal government, a resident alien. As such, I have limited rights but unlimited (it would appear) respon-

153

sibilities. I pay taxes: I checked, and in fiscal year 2002 my contributions to Uncle Sam were double the entry-level salary for a public librarian (current First Lady Laura Bush will know what that means). Over the years, my tax contributions have paid for the better part of a Tomahawk cruise missile, which may or may not be a good thing. For what it's worth, I am a law-abiding chap, generally keep my nose clean, and bag my trash neatly. But alas, I am, per your government's official classification, an alien.

I can live without voting rights. In fairness, I have not earned them, despite twelve years of honest endeavor and felony-free conduct. But my beef has to do with the way in which law-abiding, hardworking, tax-paying, limbo-dwellers like myself are treated by the system. For the record, I was invited to come to the United States to take up a position as dean at a major public research university. Indiana University asked; I came. I am not an illegal immigrant, terrorist, drug dealer, pimp, political asylum seeker, cultist, or aspiring mobster.

Once on these shores (and, indeed, before), I had to clamber through various visa hoops before embarking on the tortuous process of acquiring a green card (proof of resident alien status). I was fingerprinted in a police station. My ears were photographed at just the right angle. I dutifully completed inane questionnaires. I handed over a fistful of dollars. And then it was time to present myself (and my family) at the (not so) local Immigration and Naturalization Service (INS) office.

If you ever wondered, Mr. President, to whom the lambent words, "Give me your tired, your poor. Your huddled masses yearning to breathe free," applied, I suggest you visit your local INS branch office. For it is here that we, deans and dishwashers from all corners of the globe, are herded and processed like cattle. Arrive at the crack of dawn and you'll find that others have arrived at the crack of an earlier dawn. Grab a number (just as one does at the delicatessen counter of your local supermarket) and wait. And wait . . . in an overcrowded, overheated, and sometimes sullen room. Wait to be spoken to by functionaries, some of whose social skills make Basil Fawlty seem like Barbara Bush.

The purgatorial wait is, ultimately, followed by an interview in a back room. Blunt questions are delivered with unflinching dourness. My two-year-old son was asked by a dragon if I was, in fact, his father. Demeaned, we bite our tongues. Politically correct fools like to lambaste profiling in the context of counterterrorism, but perhaps they'd like to experience what we—the great unwashed mass of taxpaying, dragon-fearing aliens—experience on these shores. I ask you, Mr. President, do I really need to be put through such humiliation when my life is an open book?

My green card expired a year ago, so we had to go through much of this humiliating process all over again. Now, eleven months after completing all the paperwork and interviews, and after handing over yet more money, I still have not received my replacement green card. Its arrival was promised within nine months, but it has failed to materialize, and the latest estimate is fourteen months. In short, the system is broken. The INS, to quote from *The Age of Sacred Terror* by Daniel Benjamin and Steven Simon (New York: Random House, 2002), is "considered one of the most poorly administered, underfunded, understaffed, and woefully disorganized parts of government" (307). They surely did not exaggerate. Result? I am unable to leave the country to attend conferences at which I am an invited speaker. I am trapped, like a convict under house arrest, in a country that is prepared to take my tax dollars but does not treat me like a socially mature, law-abiding individual.

After many futile attempts to speak to a human at the INS Nebraska office, we were told curtly that the renewals process was taking longer than the officially promised nine months. If we needed to leave (and reenter) the country, we would have to revisit our local office once more, get in line, and do whatever was required to be granted another temporary extension. And so it was back to the local INS office (a 100-mile roundtrip), and a further wait of four hours and five minutes before a one-year exemption could be granted. But that was not the end of the saga. Ten days later, I received a missive from Nebraska explaining that the fingerprints and photos I had submitted a year earlier were unacceptable and that I would have to revisit my local INS office to be re-fingerprinted. This required a further day away from my work and a further four-hour wait for a task that took three minutes. I enquired if there were local quality controls in place to determine that fingerprints and photos conformed to INS standards, and I was told that there were not. So much, Mr. President, for customer care and procedural efficiency within the federal bureaucracy. It's a pity my hard-earned dollars weren't used to help sort out this administrative mess rather than to pay for tail fins on smart missiles.

Others have even greater grounds for complaint. As you well know, a number of resident aliens gave their lives for this country in the recent conflict in Iraq. These soldiers died for a country whose bureaucracy treats them like dirt: guilty until proven innocent, in effect. But you wouldn't know, Mr. President, because you and millions of other Americans will never know what it is like to be beyond the pale while on the inside. What you don't experience doesn't exist, even when it's on your doorstep. But the dissonance between what we aliens experience in these grim INS offices and the sparkling egalitarian rhetoric in which this nation swathes itself is simply too grotesque to be ignored.

Yours sincerely,
Blaise Cronin
Resident Alien

THE TEN BEST THINGS IN AMERICA

Willis Barnstone is one of the four best things in America. That's according to the great Argentine writer, Jorge Luis Borges. His actual words were: "Four of the best things in America are Walt Whitman's *Leaves*, Herman Melville's whale, the sonnets of Barnstone's *Secret Reader*, and my daily corn flakes—that rough poetry of the morning." Barnstone, by the way, is a distinguished professor emeritus of comparative literature at Indiana University. Reminded recently of this, I decided to come up with my own "Best Things in America" list. This seems the least one can do after unleashing a fusillade of jeremiads, often at the expense of the very nation that has been kind enough to entertain my presence for the last twelve years. So, here they are, pretty much straight off the top of my head (but also from my heart) and in no particular order.

#1. *Public Libraries*. Only joking. That was just to get your attention. For the best in public libraries, I'd have to give my vote to one of the Nordic nations. Instead, my first rosette goes to *The American Scholar*, proof that the essay genre is alive and well and that the English language is still revered by some in this country. A quarterly you long to touch and read, and a joyous antidote to the deathless prose pouring forth from university English departments. It is stylish without being precious; graceful without being anachronistic.

#2. *Richard Feynman*. We could say the same about this much loved and greatly missed theoretical physicist. Stylish without being precious, he lives on through his engaging writings and the odd television recording. The finely sculpted head, infectious smile, and clarity of thought made this bongo-playing, problem-solving Nobel laureate something special. If dons could be matinee idols, he'd have been their James Dean. Come to think of it, he was.

#3. *The New Yorker's cartoons.* Note I didn't say *The New Yorker.* That would have been too easy, too predictable. None of us in the academic game could have made it through our careers without at least once using a *New Yorker* cartoon on a purring overhead projector to make a particular point or to break the seminar ice. Urbane, pithy, and au courant—just what we all aspire to be in academe, as it happens.

#4. *The NewsHour with Jim Lehrer* (or *The McNeil/Lehrer NewsHour,* as it was formerly named). Broadcast and cable news on U.S. television is entertainment by any other name. Anchors command multimillion-dollar contracts and have become more newsworthy than many of the stories they themselves cover. Local news features soulless clones with blow-dried hair and blow-dried personalities, while CNN has degenerated into a demented collage of unqualified video clips, trite sound bites, and, of late, hip lingo and jingoism. Amidst the dross, the intelligent and civil discussions that feature nightly on the *NewsHour* are a lifesaver for this resident alien. What a contrast to the wooden rhetoric and hackneyed metaphors favored by the country's sitting president and his speechwriters.

#5. *The Beach Boys (or at least Brian Wilson) and Aaron Copland.* I don't know much about music, but Wilson and Copland have managed in their very different ways to capture the feel, smell, sights, and sounds of the edges and interior of this nation in near miraculous fashion. There may be better composers, lyricists, and performers (and there was, you're probably thinking, something called jazz), but there have been few whose music captures the topography and texture of this country with such fidelity. To listen to them is to hear America.

#6. *Night Games at the U.S. Open Tennis Championships.* The grunts, poundings, and thwacks that fill the Arthur Ashe stadium. Floodlit gladiators playing out of their skins as night envelops New York City. Titantic five-setters going on past midnight, as the Todd Martins and Pete Samprases of this world discover physical and psychic reserves of which most of us could scarcely dream. Celebs and civilians hooked until the sweat-lashed end, long past their bedtimes. Throw in John McEnroe's insightful and jauntily irreverent commentary (no wonder the BBC nabbed him for Wimbledon), and it's the perfect way to vicariously visit the Big Apple.

#7. *Transparency.* No country, no political system, is free of corruption, but some nations are absolute basket cases. For years, I've been monitoring the rankings of corrupt nations produced by Transparency International's (TI) annual survey (www.transparency.org/), and it's fascinating to see how temperate countries (e.g., New Zealand, Denmark) seem to rank so well. Even though the United States isn't exactly squeaky clean (think of Enron and countless other corporate and financial scandals), one is impressed by the relative consistency and openness, not to mention efficiency, with which parts of this country (from federal to county level) conduct their affairs. Throw in a dash of meritocracy and a soupçon of dialogic democracy, and it is a most refreshing brew, at least for those of us from the Old World.

#8. *American Universities.* The American higher education system—like every other one—has its faults: it's expensive (though, in fairness, still a great value if you look at the lifetime earning potential of graduates versus those with only high school qualifications); faculty governance is being eroded slowly, and there is much talk of progressive corporatization; the association with dubious athletic programs is becoming more, not less, embarrassing; and political correctness continues to insult common sense and infringe on individuals' constitutional rights across the nation's campuses. All of this notwithstanding, what remains is a system of unparalleled resources, remarkable intellectual vitality, and genuine diversity. No wonder we don't want to leave our (very American) ivory towers. Where else, I often ask myself, could I sit jotting with such impunity?

#9. *Are You Hot? The Search for America's Sexiest People.* I stumbled upon this ABC program by accident (what else am I going to say?) and was instantly riveted. Broadcast TV in this country is wincingly prudish and coy (like much of academia), yet this exercise in extreme exhibitionism broke all spoken and unspoken taboos. Fresh bodies appeared on stage every minute or two to be judged by a panel of three celebrities, one of whom, Lorenzo Lamas (Lorenzo who?), was introduced, not as a designer, producer, entrepreneur, or some such, but as "an international heartthrob." Now that's an unusual occupational category. Muscular young men and curvaceous young ladies traipsed semi-naked across the stage and were mercilessly critiqued in front of a baying audience in terms of their faces, their bodies, and their overall sexiness. As far as I could tell, none of this bawdy was intended to be tongue-in-cheek. "Are your boobs natural?" asked one judge. "Your nose is a little crooked," noted another with utter insouciance. But the choicest remark of all came from the official heartthrob when commenting on the sexiness quotient of a young lady in a subminimalist bikini: "I've got a burrito cookin' down south and it's almost ready." Surely, I mused, this is *Saturday Night Live* gone berserk. But no, this appallingly crass piece of television was indeed a prime-time airing on a broadcast network. How wonderfully subversive! And it was precisely that subversiveness—the producers' apparent willingness to cock a snoot at the priggishness of broadcast television in general—that I found so refreshing. For a brief moment it restored my faith in the nation, while simultaneously confirming my worst fears.

#10. *Trent Lott's Hair*. Defies comment . . . unless you're a cartoonist, in which case it pays the mortgage. Or did, until Lott's public salience went the way of most middle-aged men's hair.

About the Author

Blaise Cronin is the Rudy Professor of Information Science at Indiana University, Bloomington, where he was dean of the School of Library and Information Science from 1991 to 2003. He is concurrently a visiting professor in the School of Computing at Napier University, Edinburgh, and was also the Talis Visiting Professor of Information Science at Manchester Metropolitan University for six years. From 1985 to 1991, he was Professor of Information Science and head of the Department of Information Science at the Strathclyde University Business School in Glasgow.

Professor Cronin is the author/editor of some 300 research articles, monographs, technical reports, conference papers, and other publications. In addition, he has published numerous book reviews. Much of his research focuses on scholarly communication, citation analysis, collaboration in science, the academic reward system, scientometrics, and cybermetrics—the intersection of information science and social studies of science. He has also published extensively on topics such as information warfare, strategic intelligence, knowledge management, information marketing, distributed education, and the social dimensions of digitization. Professor Cronin is editor of the *Annual Review of Information Science and Technology* (*ARIST*), which is published by the American Society for Information Science and Technology. He was founding editor of the *Journal of Economic & Social Intelligence*, and sits on many editorial boards, including *Cybermetrics*, the *Journal of the American Society for Information Science & Technology*, the *International Journal of Information Management*, *Information Research*, and *Scientometrics*.

Professor Cronin has extensive international experience, having taught, conducted research, or consulted in more than thirty countries. Clients have included the World Bank, NATO, the Asian Development Bank, UNESCO, the Brazilian Ministry of Science & Technology, the European Commission, the U.S. Department of Justice, Chemical Abstracts Service, the British Council, Her Majesty's Treasury, Hewlett-Packard, the British Library, the Commonwealth Agricultural Bureau, and the Association for Information Management. He has been a keynote or invited speaker at scores of conferences, nationally and internationally, and lectured at fifty universities worldwide. Professor Cronin was a founding director of Crossaig, an electronic publishing start-up in Scotland, which was acquired in 1992 by the Institute for Scientific Information (ISI) in Philadelphia. For six years he was a member of ISI's strategic advisory board.

Professor Cronin was educated at Trinity College Dublin (M.A.) and the Queen's University of Belfast (M.L.S., Ph.D., D.S.Sc.) In 1997 he was awarded the degree Doctor of Letters (D.Litt., *honoris causa*) by Queen Margaret University College, Edinburgh, for his scholarly contributions to information science. Professor Cronin is a fellow of the Institute of Information Scientists, the Royal Society of Arts, the Institute of Management, and the Library Association. He can be contacted at bcronin@indiana.edu.